Afterwork

Afterwork

An Honest Discussion about the
Retirement Lie and How to Live
a Future Worthy of Dreams

Joel Malick and Alex Lippert
with Dean Merrill

AspirePress

Afterwork: An Honest Discussion about the Retirement Lie
and How to Live a Future Worthy of Dreams

© 2023 Joel Malick, Alex Lippert, and Dean Merrill. All rights reserved.
Published by Aspire Press
An imprint of Tyndale House Ministries
Carol Stream, Illinois
www.hendricksonrose.com

ISBN: 978-1-4964-7811-5

Previous edition published in 2021 under ISBN 979-8583165117.

Cover design by Cristalle Kishi, page design by Sergio Urquiza

Library of Congress Control Number: 2022043820

Printed in the United States of America
011122VP

Contents

Introduction

Many significant milestones in life are transition points ... retiring from a career, adjusting to children leaving the home, enduring an untimely job loss, suffering a major health event, stepping away from a business, or saying final goodbyes to loved ones.

Afterwork acknowledges these tectonic life transitions and offers powerful disciplines that will help you step forward into a new, remarkably fulfilling season—regardless of what you have poured yourself into in the past or how you've defined "work."

The word *retire* carries an underlying connotation of something that's old, tired, worn out, not as useful as it once was, and even obsolete. If we delve into a thesaurus, we will find synonyms such as *recede ... withdraw ... retreat ... recall ... cease ... stop.* (The British have a quaint phrase—"Become a pensioner.")

Is there anything exciting about these words? They're fairly close to clichés like "Over the hill," "Out to pasture," and "Riding off into the sunset." Birthday cards for older people often play on this stereotype with weak humor.

It's curious that when Dan Buettner set out to research our planet's "blue zones"—areas where people are most likely to live the longest and healthiest—he found that in Okinawa, Japan, "they don't have a word for 'retirement.' They talk about *ikigai*, which means 'why I wake up in the morning.' People think of themselves as being useful into their 90s and even 100s. In Costa Rica the phrase is *plan de vida*, or life plan. In blue zones, the older you get, the more revered you are. It's not like, 'Okay, Grandma, you've worked your whole life. Put your feet up.' It's more like, 'Grandma, we need you. We honor your decades of wisdom.'"[1]

In this book, we're going to try to sidestep the word *retire* in favor of more positive terms such as *your next season, the future, where you're headed*, and *the coming years*. This isn't meant to be just a word game. We truly believe you have decades of professional, emotional, and personal experience worth drawing upon.

We're also going to explore the "retirement lie," which is the false assumption that a selfish retirement is a good one. Our society has distracted us, placing too much emphasis on money and our own desires, with very little focus on what we fundamentally need. But it's a huge mistake to view the coming years as nothing more than cashing in on the money we've squirreled away—and hoping it doesn't run out before we die.

Most books you'll read on this subject say something like, "You've earned this; now here's how to make life all about you." But the truth is that you can be a lot happier than that—and a lot more fulfilled—because you were created to thrive in a purpose-breathing life.

You are not just a "What did you used to do?"; you're more resourced than ever at this stage! You have a lot more time. You have plenty of hard-earned skills and street smarts. You're likely far better off financially than in other seasons of life. And as you come into the flexibility and freedom that your accumulated assets can float, you can put your powerful talents to great use.

These attributes aid your ability to pursue your true purpose and live a life worthy of dreams. You're here to do meaningful things; it's just challenging to know where to begin. And if you approach this season the wrong way, you're going to end up a shadow of who you could have been.

So welcome to *Afterwork*. We believe that if you commit to the following ideas, you can flip the script our culture keeps trying to write out for you. We are passionate about keeping as many people as possible from feeling like their purpose and influence have expired, when the exact opposite is true.

If you want to live out your years in the most purposeful and impactful way possible, this is the book for you. Who will you be *afterwork*?

Part 1

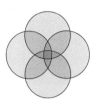

Retirement, or *Afterwork*?

Often when you think you're at the end of something,
you're at the beginning of something else.

Fred Rogers, *The World according to Mr. Rogers*

What Now?

Although for several years we'd known Carolyn,[2] a pleasant client of ours in her mid-fifties, we'd never met her husband, Bill. The day came when we finally sat down with the two of them. His graying hair bore testimony to his seniority—he'd just turned seventy—but he appeared to be in good health. His firm handshake and good eye contact let us know he wasn't shy.

Before we got down to business, one of us said in a friendly tone, "So, Bill, you've been retired for a couple of years?"

"Yes," he replied. Then out of the blue, he added, "And it's been the most challenging time of my life."

We had heard this sentiment more than once from other recently retired clients. Somehow their dreams hadn't quite come true. In this case, we didn't want to put Bill on the spot, so one of us chose to ask about his previous job. Maybe this would yield some clues to his discomfort.

How do you take a vacation when your whole life becomes a vacation?

"I was the general manager of the big Ford dealership in Palo Alto for nineteen years," he explained. "I absolutely loved it. We had so many returning customers because we did business the right way. We treated them with respect. It got to the point with a lot of these people that I didn't even have to negotiate on price, because they knew they were getting a fair deal."

"That's great," we responded. "The auto business doesn't always work that way."

"Yes, well, we created a different culture," Bill replied, warming to the subject. "I was determined to make this dealership a positive force in the community. Sure, it was hard work—ten to twelve hours a day, every day but Sunday. I lived on my feet, it seemed, meeting customers, managing staff. But I loved it."

As Bill talked, he looked off into the distance, as if to relive his past just one more time. Carolyn quietly nodded, saying nothing.

"So, what is your life like now?" we asked, turning the conversation to the present.

"Well, we've got this great property up in the Santa Cruz Mountains, at about 2,300 feet elevation. It's a gorgeous area, and we absolutely love being outside the city. It's peaceful and quiet. We had a rustic mountain-style home built just the way we wanted. We even have some redwoods up behind our place."

Apparently this beautiful setting wasn't filling the holes left by the transition. We waited to hear more.

"I spend the majority of my time maintaining this half-mile dirt road down to the highway," Bill continued. "I've got this little tractor that I fire up every time the rains wash away some of the roadbed. Gotta stay on top of the erosion. But in between times, when the sun is shining ..." He didn't quite know how to finish the sentence. His demeanor, however, seemed to ooze, *I guess I had my big season on the stage of life—and now it's gone.*

The Golden Years?

In our work as financial advisors, we've witnessed clients experiencing this kind of perplexity more than a few times. Once the conversation gets beyond their account balance, investment performance and strategy, and the documents that need to be signed, it moves toward *life satisfaction*, and we discover that many people turn out to be struggling. They wonder what they're supposed to do with all this "free time." How will they ever fill another fifteen or twenty years? It's almost as if they're asking, *Who am I when I'm not "me" anymore?*

Bill is a lot more than a road maintainer. He's a leader, a doer, a dealmaker, a developer of other people's talents. While there's nothing wrong with Bill kicking back and enjoying a quiet view of the mountains or the ocean, this in itself cannot be his narrative for the future. He's got more than enough money to pay a company to come grade his road every couple of months while he could go on engaging with people somehow. But what would that look like?

If your plan for retirement is to "do nothing" because it sounds incredible today, the problem is that your entire life may come to feel like a void once you leave your career. And you can't fill a void with "nothing."

Vacations are wonderful because they're a counterbalance to working very hard, whether you're working in the traditional sense or working perhaps even harder to raise a family. You need to take a break from all the pressure and enjoy the beach.

But how do you take a vacation when your whole life becomes a vacation? Suddenly the getaway loses its fulfillment.

People say when they retire, "I'll finally get my time back." They don't realize that time can become their largest adversary once the post-career years start to unfold.

Take a look at two graphs we constructed with data from the Bureau of Labor Statistics:[3]

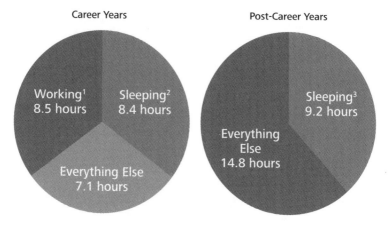

Career Years

Working[1]
8.5 hours

Sleeping[2]
8.4 hours

Everything Else
7.1 hours

Post-Career Years

Sleeping[3]
9.2 hours

Everything Else
14.8 hours

1 - Full-time employed person, average weekday hours worked
2 - Average employed American adult with children in the household
3 - Average non-employed American adult with no children in household

Throughout our career years, we're hardwired to carry the burden of so many responsibilities—our busy careers; the well-being of our families; home upkeep; car maintenance; assisting our parents as they age; remembering birthdays and anniversaries; supporting various charities; keeping up with public issues, tax laws, social expectations ... the list is long, and time is hardly enough.

Then comes that glorious, long-awaited day of retirement. All at once, the landscape lurches like an earthquake. Suddenly our free time more than doubles—we have around fifteen hours of time to fill every day.

Most people would say, "That sounds great! Can't wait. Sign me up!"

But the reality doesn't always line up with the daydream. What many of us don't understand is that when we enter *afterwork*, we leave a part of our identity behind—and that gap can't be filled with busywork.

Yet these are supposed to be "the golden years." There has to be something more, right?

"Nothing to Do"

Our collaborator on this book, Dean Merrill, tells a humorous story about one afternoon when he and his wife were trying to get their two-year-old grandson to take a nap. They were on a trip, and in the hotel where they were staying, they'd positioned a portable crib in one corner of their room. They lowered the window shades, gently put the boy down with his blanket, and then retreated to the opposite corner. Soon began the admonitions that every parent and grandparent knows all too well.

"Reuben, close your eyes and go to sleep."

"Shhh, Reuben. No more talking."

"Stop wiggling around, Reuben. Just lie still."

The child would have none of it. Too much adrenaline was coursing through his veins.

After perhaps half an hour, Dean and his wife had to stifle their snickering when they heard the little tyke bemoaning his fate in the most mournful tone he could muster:

"Nothing to do ... nothing to do ..."

More than a few retirees are muttering the same refrain these days, unfortunately. They stare out the window during the day, or at the ceiling at night, feeling untethered, useless, and bored. They wonder if they should have hung onto their previous position for a few more years. Why go on living if this is all the present can hold?

> The retirement riddle *can* be solved.

The respected Pew Research Center found that the rate of "gray divorces" (breakups for couples over the age of fifty) doubled over a period of twenty-five years. Among those age sixty-five and older, the divorce rate tripled in the same time span.[4] Additionally, numbers gleaned from six biennial national surveys revealed that "depression and depressive symptoms were significantly associated with retirement in late middle-aged U.S. workers."[5]

Yet it doesn't have to be this way. Answers are available—and most of them have nothing to do with dollar signs. The retirement riddle *can* be solved.

The "Sugar Rush"

For the first ninety days or so, the *afterwork* life seems downright blissful. The first Monday morning you don't have to deal with an alarm, you're euphoric. You can sleep in as long as you like. Tuesday morning, it's the same blessing. Wednesday ... Thursday ... Friday ...

So far, so good. You can putter around the house in your pajamas if you like. You can pull out that long-neglected list of home improvements and repairs. You can spruce up your lawn and cultivate your flower beds. You can go on an expensive vacation.

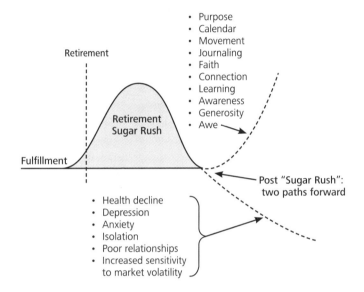

But before too many months go by, the sugar rush of retirement wears off, and then what?

Here is an honest confession: We in the retirement planning industry have missed the most critical components of your future. Our focus and analyses have been far too narrow. We've allowed you to define success as a performance return number. We've made it seem as though you're on track if you hit your savings goals. We've swamped you with charts and graphs, research reports and corporate profiles, to the point of making you blurry. Along the way, we've failed to direct your focus to what matters more.

Honestly, what's the point in getting all the financial aspects right if in the end you don't even enjoy your life? This question deserves deep reflection.

You will need a very different mindset when the "sugar rush" wanes.

The "sugar rush" isn't a bad thing. It's a very important part of the retirement transition and is meant to be enjoyed. Yet a delineation between the first months and the following years must be acknowledged. If you went to college, you well know that the first semester looked quite different than the rest of your time. If you've been married, you understand that the "honeymoon" season is special, but that's not where you live the rest of your life. If you happened to transition careers, you're aware that the onset is very different than the outset.

Enjoy this wonderful, initial season for what it is: a time to unwind, recharge, dream new dreams. But move forward knowing that you will need a very different mindset when the "sugar rush" wanes. We want to help you avoid an unexpected sugar crash.

Your Greatest Chapter

I (Joel) was speaking to a large group at a convention about this perspective, during which I said the following:

> You have value. [Notice I didn't say "had." I said "*have*."] You have capability. You have wisdom. You have financial resources. You have time. You

have experience. You've learned from many a mistake. You have persevered. This isn't your "final chapter." Instead, this can be your *greatest* chapter. Yes, it's probably the largest, most complex transition you will ever attempt in life. But you're not transitioning to a lesser version of yourself—just the opposite, if you choose. You're not a "has-been." You can absolutely become the strongest, most impactful version of you imaginable. If you haven't given it much forethought till now, it's high time to do so.

I didn't think this was such a revolutionary concept at the time. But more than one person came up afterward to say, "I never thought of it that way! Thank you so much." I began to wonder if we were on to something here. It seemed to strike a deeper chord than I had anticipated.

The coming years can surpass any whimsical journey you had hoped for. They can be a graduation of sorts, a time of widening horizons and many options. You are still useful—to yourself, your family, your society, your world. Your potential influence can be astounding.

You're a Person, Not a Portfolio

Imagine that the evening of your retirement celebration has come at last. The food is exquisite, the ambience elegant throughout the room. Photos and displays marking highlights of your career stand on easels nearby.

Your boss makes a glowing speech. Your coworkers put on a humorous sketch, or perhaps even a good-natured roast. Jokes are told, and everyone laughs heartily. Eventually, it's your turn to stand and offer a few words.

"Well, tonight I'm proud to say that after twenty-eight years with this organization, I've amassed a large retirement portfolio that will allow me to start enjoying the hard-earned fruits of my long and demanding labors."

No. You wouldn't say any such thing—and not just because it would sound pompous and self-aggrandizing. You would instead speak about the warm relationships you built, the new products and services launched by not just yourself but a whole team of people, and the appreciative notes and reviews you received from your customers and clients.

You would also thank your family members for their support through stressful times. You might even tell a story or two of how competitors showed their respect. And you would be sure to include two or three guiding principles that held you steady along the winding road.

And you would do all of this because you are a living, breathing human being. You are not just a pile of money; you're a person whose social connections are foundational to your existence. And next week, next month, next year after you leave the payroll, you will still be that person.

Getting beyond the Numbers

I (Alex) have had many discussions with a client who has always been fixated on his net worth number. "If I can reach that amount one day," he would say, "then I can be free to do what I've always wanted to do."

I finally asked him once, "Do you really think an extra comma and some zeroes are going to change how purposeful your life is or who you are"? He paused, as if he'd been struck by lightning. The fact that he'd bought into the retirement lie finally started to dawn on him.

"What's my return?" is a common question we hear when we sit down with clients to review their portfolios. They want to hear a good number. But whether you beat the market or outperform your neighbor is hardly relevant to what truly matters in building a post-career life. If you're a slave to the stock market (something completely illogical and emotionally driven in the short term), you will inevitably be tossed around like a plastic bag in a windstorm. It's unreasonable to base your view on something so fickle and volatile.

> If you're a slave to the stock market, you will inevitably be tossed around like a plastic bag in a windstorm.

A popular quote says it well: "Judge each day not by the harvest you reap but by the seeds you plant."[6] What the market does today should never be the measure of your happiness or contentment. It's a huge waste of energy.

The Fear Factor

What's driving the angst in many intelligent, successful people is actually *fear*, whether they would admit it or not. Every four years, it seems, we hear the same refrain from clients: "Well, what changes should we be considering since there's an election coming up?"

It's as if they're thinking, *If So-and-So wins the White House, that's it! The economy is doomed! We'll all fall off into the ocean!*

Another common question goes something like this: "We're probably heading into another recession, aren't we? Should we liquidate our investments and just sit on cash for now?"

We work with one couple, both in their early sixties, who have a net worth of approximately $4 million … but they tell us every year how much they both hate their jobs. "We can't wait to retire!" they exclaim. "But not now. We'd lose our health insurance."

We have demonstrated to them in many different ways how they could easily stop working tomorrow and face almost no possibility of running out of money, even if they tripled their spending and lived to be 102. They are as hedged and protected as a couple can be.

They also have children and grandkids—some are local, others out of state. When this loving pair pulls out their phones to show us pictures, their eyes light up with pure joy. But they're so occupied with work that they rarely see any of these family members face-to-face, unless it's during a preplanned get-together at Christmas or some other holiday.

Why are they so fearful? Well, there's "the coming election" and "the next recession"—plus they're not quite old enough to get Medicare. The truth is, with their nest egg, they could buy private health insurance and not even miss the money. So they continue to stay "busy" working long hours at jobs they don't enjoy, storing up more accumulated funds than they know what to do with, while their clear passion (family and legacy) is slipping through their very capable fingers. *This is a travesty.*

"Fear is the mind-killer," science fiction author Frank Herbert wrote in his famous work *Dune.* "Fear is the little-death that brings total obliteration."[7] As people churn over the what-ifs of their financial lives, fear manifests itself most often in stress. They are locked in a dead-serious battle against the unknown, that ever-lengthening stretch of post-career years and even decades. Life spans, after all, keep getting longer and longer, thanks to medical advances, improved standards of living, and other factors. A recent analysis by J. P. Morgan concludes that for a sixty-five year old married couple in good health, there is nearly a 50 percent chance that one of them will live to age ninety, and only a slightly lower chance (44 percent) that one of them will live to age ninety-five.[8]

> Fear and anxiety manifest themselves in excuses to avoid making important decisions in many seasons of life, especially surrounding *afterwork.*

From our experience, fear and anxiety also manifest themselves in excuses to avoid making important decisions in many seasons of life, especially surrounding *afterwork*. Like in the case of our client couple who wishes dearly to retire and has the means to do so, those on the cusp of life transition often let these emotions drive a lack of mental preparation, diverting their focus onto irrelevant factors. Instead of stepping out bravely into a new and better life, they inadvertently choose the status quo, even if it's not fulfilling and in fact opposite of what they truly want. We all find comfort in the known and become anxious when we encounter the unknown, whether it has a name or not.

It reminds us of that ancient account of the Israelites who were dramatically freed from slavery and started their journey toward the Promised Land. As soon as they hit a few challenges in the desert, they quickly wanted to exchange their freedom for more of their past. They whined to their leaders Moses and Aaron, "If only we had died by the Lord's hand in Egypt! There we sat around pots of meat and ate all the food we wanted, but you have brought us out into this desert to starve this entire assembly to death."[9]

The need is to be brave enough to embrace the future, understanding that it won't be easy, but it can be great. After all, how many true achievements that made us proud in our past were easy? Not many. But the freedom of the Promised Land is still superior to the bondage of Pharaoh's chain gangs.

President Franklin D. Roosevelt boldly put fear in its place in his first inaugural address (1933) amid the worst of the Great Depression: "Let me assert my firm belief that the only thing we have to fear is fear itself—nameless, unreasoning, unjustified terror which paralyzes needed efforts to convert retreat into advance."[10]

Control What Only You Can

The acronym VUCA stands for "Volatility, Uncertainty, Complexity, and Ambiguity." It is used frequently in business settings and the military to explain the world we live in. We naturally envision life and our surroundings as being orderly and logical, but in reality they are far from it. A constant flow of crises and challenging-to-comprehend developments are at odds with the tranquil and linear expectation we seem to hold in our minds of what the future holds.

> We naturally envision life and our surroundings as being orderly and logical, but in reality they are far from it.

The truth is that we are in a permanent state of flux and uncertainty, so accepting the fact that VUCA exists can help us realize how much is truly out of our control. This realization leads to a far more important understanding about what actually *is* in our control—and those are precisely the things that we need to focus on.

We can't control the cyclical nature of investment markets, the timing of recessions, the rise and fall of corporate earnings, the unexpected tragedies that happen near at hand or abroad. It makes no sense to obsess over these things. Yet in the *afterwork* world, here are some things that each one of us *can* control:

- Nurturing our relationships
- Healthy living

- Maintaining personal disciplines

- Planning ahead with life phases in mind. It's wise to take the big-picture view. (For example, from ages sixty to seventy-five, you'll probably spend more on airline tickets; after that, not so much—but you'll spend more on health care.)

- Deciding on the best living location

- How we react when adversity arises

- Determining asset allocations within our portfolios

- Managing taxes

- Making sure wills and beneficiary designations are up to date

- Best use of insurance

- Saving versus spending

We need to be intentional about our future. We can't just "let the chips fall where they may." Otherwise we may end up like the character in Hemingway's *The Sun Also Rises*, who was asked, "How did you go bankrupt?" His reply: "Two ways.... Gradually and then suddenly."[11]

The consequences of a lack of planning for the post-career season can lie dormant for years. None of us want to careen into the predicament of suddenly realizing, "Oh no! It's here!" and not have the resources we need.

But bankruptcy can hit more than just your investment accounts. We've already talked about the fact that many retirees face the conundrum of "What Now?" as they seek to find purpose in their *afterwork* life. We can't emphasize it enough—you are so much more than the assets in your portfolio.

In the next section of this book, we will delve into ten *nonfinancial* keys that, when cultivated, can make a huge difference in your future. You may find that most are not easy. But we're not selling "easy." We earnestly want you to shape your future into what it can be by approaching this season of life fully aware and with intention.

> We can't emphasize it enough—you are so much more than the assets in your portfolio.

The earlier you begin, the better the results. Just as you have accumulated financial assets over your lifetime, you can accumulate meaningful benefits over time through embracing these ten habits. Let's get busy moving you off the retirement lie and into your purpose.

Part 2

Ten Key Disciplines

Leonardo Da Vinci was 51 years old when he started to paint the Mona Lisa.

Abraham Lincoln was 52 when he became the sixteenth US president.

J. R. R. Tolkien was 62 when The Fellowship of the Ring *was published.*

Ronald Reagan was 69 when he became the fortieth US president.

Nelson Mandela was 75 when he became South Africa's first democratically elected president.

Moses was 80 when he led the Israelites out of Egypt.

You have a remarkable story ahead if you have the discipline to pursue it.

Key 1: Purpose

Little kids are infamous for pestering grown-ups with *why* questions. "Why are bananas yellow?" "Why do I have to take a nap?" "Why is the dog chasing his tail?"

But one of the biggest why questions that nags at our adult minds, especially as the years add up, is this: *Why am I here, anyway?* As we keep living, we want to do more than just pamper ourselves and "be happy."

Happiness is what we think we want. So we pursue it … but the problem is, it's often just a pursuit of self. Ultimately it can end up thwarting true fulfillment. We realize later that it wasn't at all what we wanted, and now we've wasted a lot of our most irreplaceable resource—time. (We'll talk more about this valuable commodity in the next chapter, Key 2: Calendar.)

Someone once observed that if Henry Ford had asked people "whether or not he should build a motor car, they'd probably tell him what they really wanted was a faster horse."[12] We today can behave almost as shortsightedly if we say, "If only I had a fast sports car, a better home, a beach getaway … If only I didn't have to go to work anymore." We think these things will make us happy—and when they don't, we keep looking for yet more food to feed the happiness monster.

Something greater is at stake here: meaningfulness. There is a big distinction between *happiness* and *meaningfulness*. *Meaningfulness* is a different animal that looks outward, not inward toward our surface-level self. It focuses on others—family, community, acquaintances, even strangers—whose lives we might serve and enrich. Happiness is looking to *win* something. Meaningfulness is looking to *change* something for the better.

Yes, Thomas Jefferson included "the pursuit of happiness" in the Declaration of Independence as a fundamental American right. None of us would disagree. Without this basic right, we wouldn't have freedom. However, happiness is a lagging indicator; it's not some special circumstance that you find by directly looking for it. It's more organic than that. *It blossoms out of one's purpose.*

> Happiness is looking to win something. Meaningfulness is looking to change something for the better.

When we see our purpose as larger than ourselves, we can push past the pursuit of happiness toward meaningful fulfillment (which, in our opinion, is actually an underlying requirement for true happiness). Even when hardships arise—and they will—we will withstand them better. The boat called Happiness, on the other hand, takes on water in even the smallest of storms.

Peter Drucker, the famous management guru, was well into his nineties when he told an interviewer, "My definition of success changed a long time ago.... Making a difference in a few lives is a worthy goal. Having enabled a few people to do the things they want to do—that's really what I want to be remembered for."[13]

"Busy" Does Not Equal Purpose

Time and purpose can seem to be on a seesaw, always in opposition. When your schedule is jammed and you're short of time, you assume that you're living a purposeful life. But when you have too much time on your hands, purpose can seem to ebb, becoming a recognizable deficit.

Back during the busy periods of your life, you didn't have time to reflect on whether your existence was meaningful; you were just trying to hang on and survive. But staying busy with an unending to-do list is not the same as living a purposeful life.

This applies just as much to the full-time homemaker as the business owner. Both can be swamped by their to-do lists. The clatter of daily life distracts from the pursuit of purpose.

Your plan for the future must not just be to "stay busy in retirement." Lots of busy items have no tie to a purpose. You need to retire *to* something, not just *from* something. If you're not yet prepared to do this, you're not prepared.

Before going any further, we need to say that a life purpose does not have to be cast in stone forevermore. It isn't a static thing but rather a process. It can run in seasons, during which you keep trying new things.

In other words, a sense of purpose is not a destination, a finished product you get in a chemistry lab when you mix the perfect amounts of the right substances into a glass flask. Purpose is a dynamic awareness of why you're getting up in the morning to accomplish something meaningful. That awareness may evolve over months or years—and that's all right.

Which Game Will You Play?

Simon Sinek is a brilliant British-American author who has served as a motivational speaker at venues ranging from the United Nations to the Rand Corporation to the TED stage. We heard him at the Global Leadership Summit, where he gave a presentation on "The Infinite Game." Sinek said there are two games you can play in life, whether you're running a business, raising children, or even—you guessed it—heading into your post-career years.

The *Finite Game* (think basketball or football) has a set of fixed rules. Everybody knows how many players there are, how the clock runs, and how the score is tallied. At the end, there's a clear winner. Sinek illustrated this by saying,

> I spoke at an education summit for a world-famous tech company, and it seemed to me that most of the presenters spent most of their time talking about how to beat the other big tech company. I also spoke at an education conference at this second company, where 100 percent of the presenters spent 100 percent of their time talking about how to help teachers teach and learners learn. One organization was obsessed with beating their competition; the other was obsessed with where they were going.[14]

In the *Infinite Game*, the goal is not to be the winner. There's no such thing as "best" or "first." There is only progress or lack thereof. Companies come and go, and some do better than others, but there's no finish line where all the action stops and a winner gets crowned.

Yes, competition can be helpful if it pushes us all to be better than we were. But the point is not to beat somebody else—it's to strive to be the best version of ourselves.

> The point is not to beat somebody else–it's to strive to be the best version of ourselves.

How does this relate to the post-career years? It means coming to understand that we're not playing a Finite Game. Simon Sinek ended his speech that day with this:

> Some people live their lives by the rules of the Finite Game. They wake up every day and get busy accumulating money and power. It's exhausting and stressful. At the end of life, they don't "win." They just die.
>
> In the Infinite Game, your true competition in life is yourself. Your objective each day is to become a better version of yourself. You have a cause to believe in. You live a service-oriented life. You push back daily against the human tendency to want to seek only self. Ultimately, your purpose is for others to say *they* are better because you were in their lives.

Do you find yourself naturally comparing yourself with others? Do you try to keep up with the Joneses? In fact, are you trying to *beat* the Joneses? If so, tell yourself once again that there's no trophy to win here. The only real "win" (if you need to use that term) is to leave things better than you found them. That may sound cliché, but it's true: Fulfillment will come from knowing you left your grandkids with important life lessons, not a large trust fund. It will come from the joy of watching others benefit from your generosity, not taking loads of vacations or playing golf every chance you get.

You don't "win" life; you simply have the opportunity to lead a life of meaning, and to pass that sense of meaning on to others. The mindset of comparing ourselves leads to isolation. Whether you're in first place or last place, there's always room for improvement and growth.

> Fulfillment will come from knowing you left your grandkids with important life lessons, not a large trust fund.

The Infinite Game in Action

Most retirement books, articles, and seminars portray this season of life as the time you can finally be selfish. They say things such as "You deserve ..." and "Imagine doing anything you want whenever you want to do it." The essence is that you've been working hard for the benefit of others (the company, your family members), and now it's finally *your* turn.

Wow, that's terrible advice!

What if instead you looked around for others (perhaps even in your own family) who are suffering silently? There's immense pain in every level of our society, and so much of it can be addressed with less selfishness and more benevolent action.

We are not saying you shouldn't play pickleball, hit the links, swim, or go hiking. What if when you decide to play golf, you invite a neighbor whose son or daughter is ready to give up on their marriage of fifteen years because they think they're in love with someone else? Along with chopping up the fairways, you could be dissecting the interpersonal tensions in this troubled home and finding ways to ease them. How fulfilling would that be, even if you both scored way over par? How momentous an effect could you have on everyone connected to that household (their children, for one)?

What if during the course of your week you connected with a distraught parent whose teenager is descending into the pit of drugs? You could bring up helpful resources—professional, medical, spiritual—that the parent may never have thought about employing. All kinds of vistas open up when we start seeing that the post-career years are about the Infinite Game.

Terry Bromberg had been a highly successful publisher and marketer in Los Angeles, "but it was about making a quarterly number," he says. "I made money and all that, but there wasn't a real passion there. When our daughter was about to graduate high school, I realized that after so many years helping her with homework, there was now a void in my life. People have always told me that I'm a good teacher, and I've always felt somewhat of a kinship to the underdog."

As a result, Bromberg now volunteers at an organization called Homeboy Industries, teaching math to high-risk youth and former gang members covered in tattoos. "There are days when I'm teaching, and it feels as though I'm almost having an out-of-body experience," he says. "I'm sitting over here watching me and I like what I see. It's very fulfilling when you see someone get their GED and driver's license and stay clean and want to be an accountant or something like that. Sure, we do classroom work, but we also talk about life.... Somewhere down deep, they're probably thinking, 'I don't know why that guy cares about me, because few people in my life have, but he does.'"[15]

A New Self-Identity

Isn't it interesting how, for decades in the past, people who met you would usually ask, "So what do you do?"—but after retirement the question shifts to "So what did you used to do?" This fits with the cultural motif of retirement as a world of *has-been*. Maybe they even go on to ask a second question: "How do you fill your time now?"

Stunning. Before, you were a *doer of something*— but now you're a filler of time! Who wrote *that* script? If you find yourself trying to fill time, you're definitely off course.

> If you find yourself trying to fill time, you're definitely off course.

How about changing the narrative? How about defining yourself without linking to a job, a position, or a corporate identity? How about mapping out a fresh new purpose–even if you're not retired yet! Otherwise you may wind up (once the brief sugar high wears off) searching job postings and updating your résumé for a position you don't actually want. Economists have coined a term for this U-turn: *unretirement*.[16]

Granted, some people go back into the workforce because they truly enjoy it and have talents to keep offering. Others simply need the money. But many do this out of a sense of lostness, boredom, or bereavement for what once was but is no more.

For all of us, the workplace structure plays a huge role in defining our lives. Our employers require certain duties from us, at certain times, with certain measurable criteria, resulting in certain rewards (financial but also social). When that structure comes to an end ... then what? We were hardly aware of its place in our self-definition.

What will life be like without the structure? What will be our identity and purpose after we empty the contents of our desk into a little box and carry it home along with the old plant that somehow survived the fluorescent lights all those years? Who will we be then?

Purpose Is Central

All this talk about self-identity and purpose may strike you as a bit vague. Is it really all that important? Can't you just head into retirement and "play it by ear"?

Actually, that's not a good idea. Purpose is central. If life were the solar system, purpose would be the sun, around which all the planets revolve. Do you know that it would take 1,300,000 Earths to fill up the sun's volume? In fact, the sun is 99.8 percent of the solar system's entire mass. Without the sun, everything else would fly off into the void. [17]

Without purpose, the rest of your life has no point of reference, no gravity. Yes, there are other important components of your solar system, such as the next nine keys we're going to cover in this book. But each of them, when implemented, orbits around your purpose.

As you start to articulate your sense of purpose, begin with what's most central. To give you a different analogy, imagine that you're building a new home. Where would you start?

Well, your new home definitely needs a solid foundation. It's also going to need load-bearing walls. Early on, you're going to need electrical conduits to power lights and appliances, and duct work to convey cool air in the summer and heat in the winter. None of these things are very exciting, but they set up the more glamorous features that will be added later.

If we're going to compare your life purpose to building your house and living an exciting new life from there, the starting point is not the pictures you're going to hang on the wall, or the trip to Italy for your fiftieth anniversary, or the monthly game night with your old high school friends, or the weekends you'll spend camping in the mountains.

All these things will be wonderful in due time, but first you need a foundation, and framing, and drywall on which to hang some decorations and provide a safe place to launch you into all kinds of other fun adventures. You have to build the new structure before you can walk into it and start enjoying the pretty stuff.

That, you see, is the reason for a post-career purpose.

The money you've accumulated to fund your *afterwork* is nothing more than raw lumber that will enable you to build your purpose. Earlier in your working life, you may have been too busy or too financially strapped to even contemplate this coming season. But now, it's a different story.

Reflecting on Your Purpose

So what's the next step as you seek to define your purpose going forward? We suggest carving out space for reflection—either an hour in the early morning or a few quiet minutes each night before bedtime.

But don't stop there. We have a quick story to share that illustrates the power of "kicking the tires" a bit too. When our good friend Jim was about a decade out from his estimated retirement date, he began to explore a bit. Jim had an internal, yet undeveloped sense that serving in the local prison system could be a great way to impact lives and find fulfillment. With no real sense of what that would look like in actual practice, Jim decided just to start somewhere and see where the road would take him.

> The money you've accumulated to fund your *afterwork* is nothing more than raw lumber that will enable you to build your purpose.

Fast-forward about seven years, and Jim has not only found his passion, he's also honed it. He's teaching *The 7 Habits of Highly Effective People* to inmates and is looking for ways to expand his impact now that he's in a groove and knows he loves it! Just the other day he was meeting with a graduate who had spent ten years in the system and is now out doing what Jim calls "amazing work."

By mixing in this experiment well ahead of his *afterwork*, Jim was able to give proper attention to this internal inkling, allowing it to either take root and blossom or perhaps show him it wasn't for him. Now Jim moves with confidence into this next season, knowing that when he wakes up on Monday mornings after the sugar rush has worn off, he'll have the fulfillment of a worthy challenge with massive impact potential awaiting him.

Don't be surprised if you try something and it just doesn't take. If you're still "working," there's no pressure or rush to get it nailed down right away. However, if you're already retired and not having much success in finding your "thing," discouragement can set in quite easily. So take this time to "draw the blueprints" for what you want your "house" to look like. You want to do everything you can to make sure it's sound. If you're a person who believes in God, ask him for direction at this stage—and listen for any insights he might send your way. You want to glean all the wisdom and foresight you can, right?

> Take this time to "draw the blueprints" for what you want your "house" to look like. You want to do everything you can to make sure it's sound.

In this book, we're not going to give you a set of architectural sketches to copy. You take the lead here, according to your unique personality and passions. Following are three questions to help you begin.

1. For what am I grateful?

As you survey your situation in life, what parts make you thankful? Your answers actually represent a subconscious valuation, because what you truly value is usually what you feel blessed in having.

And these blessings are most often *intangible*: Family. Health. Being surrounded by good souls. Enough earnings to cover the basic necessities of life. Beware, however, of limiting your list to just the financial, as in "I'm grateful I can afford to escape to my beach timeshare every January." Surely your blessings are more significant than that.

If you have trouble getting started with this list, think about vivid memories you hold from your working years. What were the highlights? Now go on to ask why those moments were significant. Soon you'll gain genuine appreciation for their meaning.

True gratitude bypasses the material items of our existence to reflect what our hearts cherish most—those things that spark an inner joy, a nearly unexplainable sense that we are fulfilled as we experience them.

We all have moments when someone gives us a simple smile or thank-you for investing in their life—and we get goose bumps inside. This kind of feeling is closely linked to a genuine *purpose* for our being alive. We want more of this fulfillment, whether we get paid for it or not.

2. How might I pour more of myself into these things?

From this list of people and experiences that make you grateful, you can ask yourself, *How might I pour more of myself into these things? How can I leave a lasting legacy?* (By the way, *legacy* and *financial inheritance* are not at all the same thing.)

Take the example of family. No doubt your kids and grandkids are endlessly busy with school, sports, trips, and extracurricular activities, to the point that sometimes you can't find a way to shoehorn yourself in. Yes, you all get together for birthdays and Christmas, but is that the best you can do? Why does a formal date have to be locked in for anything good to happen?

A great solution is to volunteer to drive your grandchildren to school or other activities a day or two a week. Car time is great conversation time. Or maybe you can get involved in coaching one of their sports teams, or showing them how to make something in the woodshop or kitchen. What kid doesn't like to make a yummy treat? If the goal is to enrich the life of your grandchildren, don't let the formality of appointment-setting get in the way. Be intentional and creative around the edges.

> There are many all around you whose life trajectories can be changed for the better if only you apply the tools you've spent a lifetime honing.

Ask yourself how you can offer your time, experience, or expertise, or simply your willingness to make an impact on someone you care about (whether they're a family member or not). Your unique strengths are meant to be used in this life. There are many all around you whose life trajectories can be changed for the better if only you apply the tools you've spent a lifetime honing. Your purpose does not have to be some innovative megaproject that brings you fame. It can be simple, even ordinary. But if it helps another person, and it brings you joy, it's worth pursuing.

Consider the little honeybee. If it did not pour itself into its purpose, it would lazily sit around, not pollinating anything—which would be dreadful for our food supply. Did you know that some crops, such as blueberries, cherries, and almonds, depend almost solely on honeybees for pollination?[18] Without them, the grocery shelves would be bare of these delights. The California almond industry alone needs approximately 3 million colonies of honeybees in order to pollinate its 1.5 million acres of almond orchards.[19]

Clearly, our ecosystem is finely orchestrated for purpose. But what about mankind as a whole? How sad that multiplied thousands of people retire not only from their careers but also from their contributions to others, depriving society in the process.

To quote the estimable novelist Charles Dickens, "No one is useless in this world … who lightens the burden of it for anyone else."[20] Who in your sphere of influence will thrive only as you touch their life?

3. What am I passionate about?

This third question is more personal and highly individual, of course. You are a unique person, viewing the world through a personal set of eyes. Once the necessity of a paycheck is removed from the equation, ask yourself, *What parts of my career did I really enjoy? What aspects of managing my household brought the most fulfilment? Can I keep doing these things in an altered format?*

We have a client named Paul who is passionate about crafting marketing messages. He discovered a local nonprofit that was doing great work but not telling its story very convincingly. Now he's helping the organization present itself in a more compelling light, and he's loving every minute of it.

Is there a skill or topic you've always wanted to learn more about? Maybe you can take a course at a local university. Whether you get an A or not is beside the point. The goal is to expand your horizon, engage in lifelong learning, and stretch your mind in a new direction.

And let's not forget the power of a passion that extends beyond the business world. We know a pastor in Fort Collins, Colorado—Rob Cowles—who stepped out of a well-paying executive role to start an outreach to broken people: the addicted, the victimized, those with criminal records. His new church, called the Genesis Project ("space for people to discover new beginnings"), is swarming with ex-cons, biker dudes, women who have escaped the sex trade, you-name-it. In his book, *The God of New Beginnings*, Rob writes, "When I talk about the work these days, I sometimes get frustrated when I choke up. But I've never been happier in my life, and neither has Joy [his wife]. I told her long ago, 'I simply have to be part of something that makes me cry when I talk about it.'"[21]

Your New Job Description

> Frame your own purpose statement and let it become your North Star for the future.

Over the past years of your working life, you've no doubt been given more than one job description; if you were in management, you drafted these documents for your subordinates. But now it's time to write *your own* job description for the coming years.

Having asked the preceding three questions, you can now take up the challenge of spelling out your major values, activities, and outcomes. Frame your own purpose statement and let it become your North Star for the future. Yes, it would be good to commit it to actual text (on paper or a screen), where you can see it and revise it, improving it tomorrow or next week or next month. But as you start to live out the sense of purpose you've written for yourself, be mindful of a couple of sobering realities.

First, prepare yourself for hardship. There will be unpleasant surprises. Things won't always run smoothly. Life won't roll out the red carpet for you at every turn.

Rasmus Ankersen, a Danish entrepreneur and student of high-performance culture, tells a story about visiting the MVP Track and Field Club in Kingston, Jamaica.[22] As every running fan knows, the Jamaicans are incredible sprinters throughout world competitions.

The coach at this club, Stephen Francis, agreed to show Ankersen around and told him to show up for the 6 a.m. practice. Ankersen arrived early, at 5:30, looking for a state-of-the-art training facility. Instead, he found himself staring at a worn-out field and shabby gymnasium. Had he gotten the directions wrong?

No! Stephen Francis soon appeared to explain that, while he strives to provide athletes with what they need, he also asks something of them in return. "I want an environment that tests people and gives me the answer to what I believe is the most important question: Who wants it most? This place is not designed for comfort but for hard work," he said. "If you're driven by comfort and glamour, you won't want to come here. But if you really want to improve—to do better today than you did yesterday—then this club is the place to be."

One of Francis's success stories is Asafa Powell. No American college had come to scout him during high school or offer a scholarship, despite Jamaica's reputation for fast runners. Powell, at six feet three and weighing 194, was too bulky to be a sprinter. But when Stephen Francis decided to work with Powell anyway, he searched the island until he found a hundred-meter stretch of roadway with a steep *10-percent grade* (rarely do you find an American highway with more than a 5- or 6-percent grade). He then put Powell to work on this brutal slope.

This may have something to do with the fact that the adult Asafa Powell has gone on to break the ten-second barrier *ninety-seven times* in the hundred-meter race, and that he won a gold medal at the 2016 Summer Olympics as part of the Jamaican 4 x 100–meter relay team. He also holds the world record for the 100-*yard* dash at 9.07 seconds.

Stephen Francis has one ruling principle that can be applied to any of us: *Hunger is more important than skill.* If you tell yourself you're just a normal person who probably isn't going to make much of an impact in the coming years, you probably won't. But if you're eager to live a purpose-filled life, you can.

It all comes down to hunger … desire … or to use an even stronger term, *grit*—the determination to forgo comfort as you get busy pursuing impact, day in and day out. You don't have to be an exceptional talent with a lengthy résumé of past achievements. You don't need to hope for "the breaks" along life's future path. You simply need grit.

We recently listened to a podcast by Jordan B. Peterson, the Canadian clinical psychologist who was dubbed "the world's most influential public intellectual."[23] He's an author and professor emeritus at the University of Toronto, as well as a former professor at Harvard.

In his informal and conversational style, Peterson shared his clinical observations on the need for meaning in life—and framed it within the context of work structure:

> People [struggle] if they don't ... slot in somewhere.... You think, ugh, I've gotta go to work at nine in the morning and, you know, I've got this rigid schedule....

> It's probably a good idea to be grateful for that. Because what I have noticed is that if people pull out from those externally scaffolded systems ... they get depressed. They get anxious. They don't know what to do with themselves.

> You know, they're kind of like sled dogs with no sled. And we're kind of like sled dogs as far as I can tell ... beasts of burden.

> Like, we need a load, man. We need a load. And the question is, What sort of load do you need?[24]

When a clinical psychologist like Dr. Peterson draws a conclusive observation about the concept of drift, we should take note. *Afterwork* is going to be a challenge, and that's okay. As Peterson observes, we are built to carry a load.

If we can face this season head-on, with the right posture and mindset, we can ascend to meaningful summits. However, if we are expecting something easy, we'll be sorely disappointed.

What's your "sled?"

Second, beware of "retirement drift." Our lives are always in danger of drifting from our spiritual or moral or performance standards. We slack off on things like aspiring to grow in our marriage or friendships, or hitting the gym as much as we should. We get distracted with other, more pleasurable pursuits.

> If we can face this season head-on, with the right posture and mindset, we can ascend to meaningful summits.

Our best-laid plans for the future are vulnerable to drift over time. The ancient Chinese philosopher Lao Tzu warned us in his clever saying, "If you do not change direction, you may end up where you were heading." Is that really what we want?

Here's an example to consider. Have you ever tried placing a line of orange cones for your child's athletic practice in the park? You walk forward, dropping one cone after another in what you're sure is a straight line … until you get to the corner of the playing field. You turn around to admire your work, and sure enough, the line is crooked! *How did that happen?* you ask yourself. *I'm sure I walked straight!*

If on the next try you turn around and walk backward so you can see the cones you've already laid out, your line will probably be straighter, but the cones will likely still be angling off in an unwanted direction. So what's the solution?

What every youth coach needs is a plumb line—a tree or post at the edge of the field to aim toward. It won't move. As long as you keep heading for that marker, your line of cones will be accurate.

If you set your course for the coming years according to a clear purpose, and muster the grit to pursue it daily, come what may, you will achieve meaningful fulfillment. Your life will count for something valuable, and you'll be happy with the result.

What course will you set for finding your purpose?

Key 2: Calendar

In the previous chapter, we covered *what* to do in the days and months and years ahead—activities that are purposeful and meaningful, not just time-fillers.

In this chapter, we turn to the question of *when* to do those things.

Life up to now has been filled to the brim with structure, both at work and in the child-raising years at home. We've been telling ourselves, *Okay, I need to get up at 5:45 every morning in order to _____ before I head out the door.*

Once at our places of employment, we loaded up our calendars with weekly meetings, deadlines, and travel. When we returned home, the kids needed to be fed, to do their homework, and to get to bed at a certain hour.

This has been your life, year after year. With only a certain number of available hours, you've had to constantly plan ahead and prioritize. But once you "retire," most of the structure vanishes, as we already touched on in the previous chapter.

These days you can sleep in as late as you want. And team meetings in the conference room? Who cares! As we said in the first chapter, you now have twice as many waking hours to use as you wish.

Some people think it's silly to keep a calendar in retirement, because they have complete freedom to do—or not do—anything.

What does not change for most of us, however, is the inner drive to stay organized. If we somehow feel disorganized, a sense of stress begins to well up inside.

Have you ever walked into a friend's or relative's cluttered garage, messy storage room, or disheveled pantry, and started to feel uneasy? Tools, boxes, and "stuff" are lying around haphazardly everywhere you look. If you wanted to find a simple screwdriver, or a can of beans, you'd hardly know where to start. *Wow, how can someone live like this?* you murmur to yourself.

Well ... what if someone could track your post-career or empty-nest life for a week? What would they see? Would it seem disorganized and random? Would cobwebs be forming in important areas?

Manage Your Calendar

Time (like money) can greatly benefit us if we *manage* it. The details now will be different from the past, of course. Even the format of our calendars (physical or digital) may be different. But the value remains high. If there's no base from which to begin, your whole life becomes a tangle of loose ends.

The point is not to fill every box, every hour with busyness. That is as much of a trap as not managing your calendar at all. If you fill your days with unending "noise" that isn't aligned with your purpose, you will miss the mark. And if you're a list-maker, you may momentarily feel good that you checked off all the items for a given day, week, or month. But what did it all mean in terms of your personal purpose? Some people sit on an organization's board for no better reason than "that's what retirees do," rather than being committed to their mission and contributing valuable input.

Some people are in the groove of writing a new to-do list every few days, copying over the unchecked items from the previous list so they'll be sure not to miss anything. But if the tasks are hollow, this self-congratulation wears thin. Sooner or later, the *why* of the activities must be confronted.

> The point is not to fill every box, every hour with busyness. That is as much of a trap as not managing your calendar at all.

Activity definitely has its benefits. Along with one of his grad students, Dr. Sheldon Cohen, a psychology professor at Carnegie Mellon University, conducted a study of older adults who had volunteered at least two hundred hours over the prior year. They found greater increases in their psychological well-being—and even lower blood pressure!—than among non-volunteers. "Even commuting to volunteer sites and activities," they wrote in the journal *Psychology and Aging*, "may also increase physical activity, therefore decreasing hypertension risk."[25]

But the activity has to be planned, scheduled, and controlled. In our practice, we have some go-getter clients who are hard to schedule for even a one-hour annual financial review in our office. "I'm too busy," they protest. They've packed their days and weeks with one activity after another, nonstop, because they're afraid of waking up one morning with nothing to do. That's not *managing* a calendar.

The goal is to strike a balance between service, rest, reflection, new experiences, disciplines, and connection. It is to structure your week or day in advance so you move forward intentionally, not just leaving each day up to chance.

A different client of ours has the right idea, we think, by blocking out time every Tuesday to visit his adult kids and simply fix things they haven't gotten around to—or don't know how to fix. What a great service to busy parents who are working full-time and raising kids. This client has also established times to read, write, and create art. His structured, well-thought-out calendar helps him tremendously in his effort to remain on the path of purpose.

We heard about one pastor who made sermon preparation such a priority that, when cornered after church by someone who wanted to see him on, say, Wednesday morning, he would pull out his pocket calendar, take a quick look, and then reply, "Oh, I'm sorry—I have an appointment that morning. I'll be glad to see you a different time, though." The parishioner never knew that the pastor's prescheduled Wednesday "appointment" was with the writings of the prophet Isaiah or the apostle Paul! A managed calendar was keeping the pastor on track in that moment, protecting his calling.

Mornings Are Strategic

A good calendar must begin with quelling the worries that can often flood in after waking up and thinking about the upcoming day's realities. To kick-start your day and gain traction up front, try to engage in at least two of the following activities, moving among the four throughout each week:

1. Physical movement (we'll unpack this in the next chapter, Key 3)
2. Journaling (Key 4)
3. Spiritual growth (Key 5: Faith)
4. Reading or listening to something inspirational or creative (Key 7: Learning)

All of these contribute to serious momentum and silence the internal voice that tells you you're tired and not good enough anymore, the internal critic that asks, *What's the point anyway?*

The rest of your morning should then be structured to manage your *energy* as well as your *time*. When are you the sharpest, the most creative, the most energized? For most people, the answer is morning. You can do more critical and creative thinking earlier in the day. This is "prime time."

A long-forgotten sage once observed, "Each season of life has its unique shortage. For the first twenty-five years of your life, your shortage is *money*. For the next twenty-five years of life, you hopefully have more money—but now you're short of *time*. And then you get to the third twenty-five years of life, when you have adequate money and definitely more time—but the shortage instead is *energy*."

If that's true for you, it's necessary to maximize the energy you still have. If one of your goals is to learn more about a certain period of American history, morning is the time to engage with this material. If you happen to love art and want to create illustrations for children, this is the time to get out your easel or sketch pad. If you've volunteered to write a strategic policy paper for the nonprofit where you volunteer, this is the time to get busy at your computer. You'll not only be more efficient at completing your meaningful aims but will also feel better later in the day knowing you've already done some heavy lifting.

What you do *not* want to do when you get up in the morning is hop onto Facebook, scan emails, see how the stock market is doing, or surf TV channels! The very last thing you need is for Wall Street or Washington, DC, to tell you how to feel today.

> What you do *not* want to do when you get up in the morning is hop onto Facebook, scan emails, see how the stock market is doing, or surf TV channels!

Don't burn energy on things you can't control. They will color your thoughts for the rest of the day, keeping you from applying valuable time and energy on something that actually matters and will make a difference.

We're not saying you should stick your head in the sand and ignore what's going on in the world. But don't give the gathering of news information a place in "prime time." Treat it like you would lawn mowing or car maintenance: something to get to later in the day, when your focus and energy have already been applied to purposeful endeavors.

Are we ruling out a "lazy morning" once in a while? Not at all; those are fun. But if you have seven lazy mornings in a row, they just turn into … mornings. Something can be "lazy" only in contrast to "non-lazy." And in the end, that's what you want.

A Blueprint for Your Day

If you desire an outline for a well-designed day, here's our recommendation:

- First, as we've already discussed, kick-start your momentum with two of the following, cycling through all four throughout the week:

  1. Physical movement

  2. Journaling

  3. Spiritual growth

  4. Reading or listening to something inspirational or creative

- Second, create something; learn something; think through an important challenge.

- After lunch, get some of the mundane chores off your list.

- As evening approaches, prepare for a meaningful connection with family or friends over dinner.

This isn't rocket science by any means, but it gives you a tremendous advantage as you pursue your purpose day after day.

Seasons and Texture

On a broader scale, we can greatly benefit from being aware of our post-career seasons—periods of months that are different from those that came before or will come in the future.

If you live in a climate that has four distinguishable seasons, you know that each one has a certain texture or flavor and is marked by its own unique activities. Some things you do outside in the warm summertime, and others fit better in winter.

If your life doesn't have seasons, then you don't have markers—moments when you consciously take stock, noting progress, achievements, and fulfillment. You need times to look at your life and say to yourself, *I accomplished this, and I'm proud of it. Now I'm going to turn my attention to _____.*

Including vacations in your calendar is especially valuable for capturing the larger picture. It allows you to get out of your normal setting and see things you'd missed along the way. You realize what brought you joy and where you got sidetracked. You start making plans for what will be different and better once you return home. And you remind yourself that you don't need to be busy all the time—you can embrace silence. Throughout your calendar, it could actually be useful to set aside times for silence. If you don't, you'll find that your aspirations for quiet reflection never quite seem to happen. Give yourself permission to sit quietly. Life was never meant to be slavery to the to-do list.

> Give yourself permission to sit quietly. Life was never meant to be slavery to the to-do list.

Calendar is a way of marking the ebb and flow of your day, your week, your year. It's about structuring themes that create fulfillment. A calendar helps you assess whether the many parts and pieces of your life are actually aligning with your goals, priorities, and purpose. Let your calendar reflect the best version of you, providing structure for what you're called to do in this most wonderful season of your life.

Key 3: Movement

When we sit down with a client, our first topic of conversation is not normally the hard numbers of their portfolio or their investment strategy. Instead, we ask about how they're doing and what's new in their life, and often we ask them to tell us about their last fun travel experience.

Dave and Barb were glad to share highlights from their recent excursion to Europe with their kids and some of the grandkids. It wasn't cheap, but they'd saved for it along the way. The trip had been a longtime goal; they'd always preferred to spend their assets on experiences instead of things.

As they described their experience, we saw them both light up. However, when the conversation turned to plans for the next year, it became apparent they were coming to grips with the possibility that this trip may have been their last one—not because of finances, but because of their physical health. They admitted they didn't feel strong enough to attempt something like that again.

As we age, medical issues often keep us from certain activities we'd like to keep doing; but we really shouldn't let ourselves feel too badly if we simply can't engage in as much movement as we'd like. After all, that's normal.

Yet the fact of the matter is that Dave and Barb *could* have stayed more active over the last decade to keep themselves in much better physical shape, and they chose not to. To live an active life now seemed like an impossible hill to climb. It begged the question, *How many future trips and memories with family would they be forfeiting?*

It's All Relative

If you're getting uneasy with this chapter's topic, please relax. Hear this important statement: *Exercise or movement is a completely relative undertaking.* We're not going to browbeat you into becoming an ultra-marathoner. Put out of your mind any image of Forrest Gump running back and forth across America for three years!

Something as simple as a brisk walk through the neighborhood can start to produce remarkable results in your life. Whatever your health or circumstance, you can benefit from a more active, movement-filled existence.

The point is not to outperform somebody else you know but to gradually increase your capacity for a healthy existence. This stage comes with certain aches and pains you didn't have to navigate earlier in life, but don't let those annoyances stop you from finding a routine that works.

I (Joel) am extremely proud of my mom, who had to deal with debilitating sciatic pain in her lower back and legs. A terrific client, who also happened to be a physician, suggested that she find a good exercise bike since walking was unbearable. She committed herself to it and loved the daily quiet time and routine—which also happened to substantially help her pain. The key is that my mom did what she could with what she had.

Temporary Discomfort Creates Lasting Comfort

The next statement may sound contradictory, but it's true: *Temporary discomfort creates lasting comfort.* What we mean is that what you foresee as being uncomfortable or challenging can in fact be worthwhile. When discomfort stems from challenging yourself in new ways, it actually creates comfort long-term. Thus, the way to experience true comfort is to be "comfortable" with being uncomfortable.

Exercise, which is often uncomfortable, is a perfect example of this inverse relationship. Your heart beats faster than your resting rate, your lungs are forced to come alive under the exertion, your pores sweat, and muscles start to burn ... you're definitely uncomfortable.

> The way to experience true comfort is to be "comfortable" with being uncomfortable.

But how does it feel when you finish exercising? You're glad it's behind you, but you also have a sense of satisfaction that you put in the effort. A few days or weeks later, you start to notice that stairs are slightly less burdensome, and lifting grocery bags is a little less strenuous. You find yourself able to stay on your feet longer. This slow but noticeable progress over time is enormously meaningful to your mental confidence and self-worth.

Getting up on our feet and becoming more active is a way to chalk up small victories. If you start with five-minute walks and later in the year realize you're walking a mile or two and feeling great ... that breakthrough will bring a smile within you.

It's real success, not because it measures up to societal or cultural standards, but simply because you know *you* have improved. You feel better, and you remember all the steps it took to reach this new lofty point. Then, a year later, perhaps you're slowly jogging a bit.

Each milestone becomes a challenging summit to reach and glean satisfaction from. The first summit begets the next, and so on. You keep telling yourself, *I'm getting better; I'm becoming healthier. I can do more activities with my children, grandchildren, and friends. My temporary discomfort is producing lasting comfort.* Some people wonder how anyone could have the stamina to run a marathon. The answer is that it develops as they continue to challenge what they previously believed to be impossible. Eventually they wake up one morning with the ability to run twenty-six miles.

Benchmarking our current selves against our former selves is the path to fulfillment. Laying aside the relentless pressure to compare ourselves to others is the only way to achieve true accomplishment. As Simon Sinek cleverly states in his book, "Better is better than best." What he means by that is, you're not doing this to be "the best," so just relax. You're not trying to win the award for "Most Strenuous Worker-Outer." You don't need to run more miles than Jill, or show up earlier than Doug. This is a battle to become a better *you*.

Collateral Benefits of Movement

The more you move, the more you start to notice positive effects. Your blood pressure drops, you're less stressed, you have time for self-reflection, and you can better your relationships because you're more grounded. You feel a sense of accomplishment on many fronts. The collateral benefits of movement include, but are certainly not limited to, the following important aspects of your life.

Physical Health

With regular activity, it's possible that you'll visit your doctor less often and spend less at the pharmacy. You might even find you can make it through winter without getting bogged down by colds and other sicknesses. And who would have guessed that consistent physical movement fights against the potential loss of some of your most precious assets: your memory and the ability to think for yourself? One scholarly study states,

> The beneficial effects of regular physical activity on health are indisputable in the field of modern medicine.... According to a US Department of Health and Human Services report on physical activity, regular exercise significantly reduced causes of mortality by up to 30% for men and women.... These health benefits are seen consistently across all age groups and racial/ ethnic categories....
>
> In addition ... regular exercise and physical activity lowers prevalence of chronic disease(s).... Individuals who exercise regularly exhibit slower rates of age-related memory and cognitive decline in comparison to those who are more sedentary.[26]

Relaxation

A Harvard Health Publishing article carries the unusual title "Exercising to Relax." It says in part,

> The mental benefits of aerobic exercise have a neurochemical basis. Exercise reduces levels of the body's stress hormones, such as adrenaline and cortisol. It also stimulates the production of endorphins, chemicals in the brain that are the body's natural painkillers and mood elevators. Endorphins are responsible for the "runner's high" and for the feelings of relaxation and optimism that accompany many hard workouts—or, at least, the hot shower after your exercise is over.[27]

Movement and exercise helps you step away, albeit briefly, from the proverbial grind of life and allows you to live in the now.

To put it another way, the next time you find yourself stressing about the news headlines, the investment markets, global macroeconomic trends ... try redirecting that energy toward movement. You may soon be in the best shape of your life—and worrying less.

But there's more ...

Living in the Now

Movement and exercise helps you step away, albeit briefly, from the proverbial grind of life and allows you to live in the now—a much researched and followed practice. Being present in this exact moment helps clear your mind of the never-ending clutter of to-do lists, as well as useless emotions and nonbeneficial self-talk. It helps you experience life to the fullest in this very second.

Constantly focusing on the future instead of living in the "now" is undoubtedly one of the reasons why time seems to pass too quickly. When the future arrives, our new focal point once again becomes the future, without much regard to the present second, the present breath we are inhaling.

Movement is never redundant, even if you wear the same jacket and shoes and choose the same route when you take a walk. Each occasion is unique, and your thoughts, circumstances, and body are always changing. Every time you get on your feet and move, it's a new experience.

Many runners listen to music to distract their minds from the discomforts of heavy breathing and sweating. But in so doing, they can miss the "now-ness" of the activity. There's nothing wrong with an inspirational podcast or song, which can be a great respite. But the next time you exercise, try to have no stimuli besides your own mind. After some practice, you may find more comfort within that space than you ever thought possible.

Real Effort, Real Results

All of us would have to admit that in many facets of life we've coasted through a situation or potential challenge without exerting much real effort—only to find that cheaply obtained results weren't results at all. If we had invested true work, we would have been happier with the outcome. Phillips Brooks, a renowned Boston clergyman in the late 1800s, said, "Do not pray for easy lives. Pray to be stronger men!"[28]

We have to be honest and state that exercise always takes effort. But even if you jog slower than normal, your body and mind are still benefiting. Active lifestyles naturally move us toward real results by design, because every step, every lift, every exerted breath is a challenge.

Isaac Newton's First Law of Motion applies well here: An object at rest remains at rest. Change only comes when you force your "object" (your body) to get up from its static state and start moving. If you allow your body to settle into inertia, it takes effort to interrupt that state. But once you do, the rewards will be priceless.

Aging Young

There are those in midlife who love to extol their position as "getting old" or "feeling their age." These people tend to be wrinkled, tired, and stationary—well before they would ordinarily be deemed old by society, or at least appear to be old on the surface. They're the grandma-and-grandpa types who look the part but don't even qualify yet for the senior discount!

Then there's the opposite—folks in their seventies and even eighties who have signed up for a 5K race or are heading out for a hike. The contrast is striking.

What's the difference between these two types of people? The latter have decided to "age young" by engaging in movement.

Excuses abound among the sedentary: "I have a bulging disc ... My knees are bad ... My hips are bad ..." But the truth is, no matter what your health situation, a more active lifestyle (unless clearly restricted by your doctor) will make you younger and healthier.

The Silhouette in the Window

Every time I (Alex) am out on a run and pass a hospital or assisted-living facility, a renewed sense of mortality strikes me. I suspect that dozens of people are looking out those windows, watching me run by. It's possible they're yearning to go for a jog as well instead of struggling with health challenges or even nearing life's end.

In those moments of being observed, I'm overwhelmingly grateful for my ability to get outside, inhale the fresh air, and run down the street. It always strikes an emotional chord for me.

If we have the *ability* to be active, thereby improving our lives through exercise and movement, don't we have an inherent responsibility to do just that? In our opinion, the answer is yes. As Marvel comic book creator Stan Lee famously wrote in his Spider-Man comics, "With great power comes great responsibility." This applies in so many areas of life, including physical activity.

> One day *you* may be the silhouette in the window, watching another person enjoying an active life and wishing you could join in.

So don't hesitate another day to get up and start moving—not only for yourself but also for all those who can't. Enjoy the bliss they can only dream of.

Sure, it takes effort. But one day *you* may be the silhouette in the window, watching another person enjoy an active life while wishing you could join in—but alas, that opportunity will have passed.

Remember, a brisk run doesn't need to be your objective. Pushing yourself comes in all shapes and sizes, but the benefits are universal. So get up and live the life you want. It's right there; you just have to move to get it.

Key 4: Journaling

The minute you saw this chapter title, what stereotype went through your mind? An older, aristocratic lady with plenty of time on her hands, writing down her various emotions? A grade-school child scribbling in a diary with a lock, then hiding it under the bed? If so, you've not explored the half of it.

Hal Elrod, a popular podcaster and best-selling author, says in his book *The Miracle Morning*, "Writing in a journal each day, with a *structured*, strategic process ... allows you to direct your focus to what you did accomplish, what you're grateful for, and what you're committed to doing better tomorrow. Thus, you more deeply enjoy your journey each day, feel good about any forward progress you made, and use a heightened level of clarity to accelerate your results."[29]

We consider journaling to be a sister to movement, the topic of the previous chapter. Whereas exercise is a physical action, journaling is a workout for your mind and emotions. At the start, writing in a journal may seem more rudimentary, but if you keep going, you will find you not only enjoy it but also need it.

> Journaling is a workout for your mind and emotions.

J. M. Barrie, the Scottish novelist and playwright (best remembered for creating the character Peter Pan), said it well, "The life of every man is a diary in which he means to write one story, and writes another; and his humblest hour is when he compares the volume as it is with what he vowed to make it." Only when we write down our reflections can we make these comparisons.

Later in this chapter, we'll explain more about how to effectively journal. But with that said, we think the process is more important than the product. Just as we didn't lay out a seven-point exercise plan in the last chapter, we won't go so far as to say you need to write this or that in order to benefit. We'll offer some suggestions to help you kick off a meaningful life of journaling, but it's up to you to discover it for yourself.

We *will* tell you right now that your first journal won't resemble your fifth one. This is because, as you walk through life's ups and downs over time, you'll tend to write the content you find most helpful.

No one is here to judge you. Some entries will be better than others, and there will be lots of times you don't feel like journaling (just like any useful discipline). That's okay; do it anyway! Your journal is one of the few places you can go to *just be you.*

How Does Journaling Help?

Journaling helps you self-reflect. Hectic lives leave little room for true consideration of your day. It's interesting how many little victories and lessons can be lost along the way unless you take the time to write them down. The journaling process is one of introspection, taking the time to revisit your day or some complex occurrence, then mentally invest in scrutinizing what transpired. To remember but also to learn so your future self is that much better.

I (Joel) was recently in conversation with a reader of an earlier edition of this book who had started journaling. He was fascinated by how each of his entries eventually concluded with "Today was a good day." He went on to add that prior to this, the negatives of the day would dominate. But when written down and processed, he could more clearly see that all his actions, fears, desires, disappointments, and challenges generally ended up in a better light after journaling and reflecting.

Award-winning poet and filmmaker Julia Cameron coined writing as life's "windshield wipers."[30] Think of the wipers as clearing out the clutter in your mind. Having a place to write about the things that occupy your thoughts paves the way for you to be more effective.

You may assume that we human beings think at the same rate as we speak, but we don't. Our brains are much faster than our mouths. We communicate verbally at roughly 150–200 words per minute and talk to ourselves at approximately 1,300 words per minute. [31]

> Having a place to write about the things that occupy your thoughts paves the way for you to be more effective.

And unfortunately, most of our self-talk is negative. It can be beneficial to just dump what's racing around the inside of your mind by writing about it and reflecting on it. This leads to a cleaner windshield, so you can more effectively reach your goals for the day and stay out of a long debate with all your nagging thoughts.

Do you prefer driving with a clean windshield or a dirty one? Socrates was right when he said more than two thousand years ago, "The unexamined life is not worth living."

Journaling is the least-expensive form of counseling. Let's face it: Life is a ball of emotions. It's hard and beautiful and messy and tiring and terrible and awesome. Writing helps you decompress and think more clearly about the issues you face, similar to the way that talking through a problem with a trusted friend or family member can help you better prepare to address it.

> Writing helps you decompress and think more clearly about the issues you face.

You know how there are times when something bad happens that elevates your blood pressure, and you really shouldn't respond right away? Taking the additional step of writing down what you're experiencing can bring the breakthrough you're looking for on how to respond to or handle a situation. Getting the problem out of your head and onto paper lightens the load, helps you think constructively, and affords you some freedom to get on with your life instead of stewing on the matter for days.

The act of unloading or decompressing all of our complex emotions in real time also helps avoid emotional buildup that can cause issues in the future. Yes, of course you could choose to share your deepest feelings and fears with a trusted confidant, or if you wanted to pay for professional services, you could see a psychologist or counselor. They serve important roles that we don't want to dismiss.

Yet there's also no denying that journaling is like having your own personal therapist. Here you can uncork your raw, extremely personal emotions and release the pressure that has built up within yourself.

Journaling can shift your perspective. Sheryl Sandberg, former longtime COO of Facebook, lost her husband in 2015 from unexpected heart failure. During this valley, she turned to writing. Before she went to bed each night, she journaled about three moments when she found joy during the day. [32] And it changed her life, shifting her perspective to joy and gratitude. Here's what she said about this period of grief during a commencement speech:

> It is the greatest irony of my life that losing my husband helped me find deeper gratitude— gratitude for the kindness of my friends, the love of my family, the laughter of my children.... My hope for you is that you can find that gratitude— not just on the good days, like today, but on the hard ones, when you will really need it. [33]

Sandberg's words are a great example of how journaling lets you take stock of those easily overlooked but brilliant pieces of life that are precious.

Journaling fosters creativity. Whether you're unpacking new ideas or simply writing what's on your mind, writing is a creative act that reduces stress. You are crafting your story. You are documenting your journey along the way.

When the word *creative* comes up, people tend to think of artists, graphic designers, writers, and painters. But as Stefan Mumaw, an author of several books on creativity, puts it, "Creativity is a skill, and any skill that you can undertake, the byproduct to it being a skill, is that you can get better at it." [34] An artist can be creative, but so can a mom, a mathematician, a salesperson, a CEO, or a retiree.

Creativity is so important because it helps you become a better problem solver. As you journal your way through various issues, you come at them differently than you would by just chewing on them within your mind. And once you see problems as survivable, you're more willing to enter unknown situations, confident that you can overcome any issue.

An artist can be creative, but so can a mom, a mathematician, a salesperson, a CEO, or a retiree.

Journaling creates a "written photo." Photos bring smiles to our faces and help us remember the past, whether it's the places we've visited or family gatherings through the years. Journaling is a complement to the old photo album, telling the stories that pictures can't.

These precious nuggets can be used in many ways: They can bring joy as you reflect on past conversations with a child, parent, or spouse. They can be used by others to find strength and encouragement in an area of life where they're struggling. They can also add valuable details to your story that would otherwise be forgotten.

For example, the two of us would love to go back and read about some of the conversations we had with our parents and grandparents when we were younger. Unfortunately, nothing was ever written down, so we look at the pictures and wonder what life was like behind the photo. What were we struggling with? What were we thinking about? What was good or bad?

A few years back, I (Joel) took a day off to go on a field trip with my oldest daughter. We headed

120 miles southeast to Bent's Old Fort National Historical Site. Constructed in 1833 along the Santa Fe Trail, it played a major role in opening the West. Trade fostered relationships between diverse people groups, and their lives were forever changed.

There are no photographs, of course, of Bent's Fort in its heyday. When you're visiting a place like this, you want to believe it's true to its original state. You find yourself imagining the people in the rooms. What was life like without such basic necessities as a light switch? How did they build all their own equipment with fire and steel? Was Amazon delivery, like, *four* days back then?!

The original fort has long since crumbled, and building the replica took fifty-six years, consisting of alternating disappointments and triumphs and the persistent hopes and untiring work of many people. How did they do it? The rebuilders relied on descriptions. Fortunately, there was a sketch of the fort in the journal of Lt. James Abert, an Army topographical engineer. He arrived at Bent's Fort in 1846 and spent several months there while recovering from an illness. Abert's careful drawing featured many details, including the fort's dimensions and room layouts.

My daughter and I toured each of the rooms, and they were all intriguing. But the most special for me was the room where his journal was on display. It wasn't easy deciphering his cursive handwriting, but the information was priceless. Can you imagine if he hadn't written it down? Imagine if Lewis and Clark didn't keep a journal either!

Of course it's easy to look at this example and say, "Yeah, yeah, but we're not conquering the West. I'm just trying to get through dropping the kids off at school and handling all the day's emails!" You're correct—and I bet the pioneers didn't see heading out to hunt each day as interesting. After all, it was as rudimentary as driving to work.

Whether you're just trying to make an impact on your kids, help friends and family around you, perhaps start a business, or keep a record of your life's challenges, the details you record are unique and valuable—and they will likely grow in value as time marches on.

> The details you record in your journal are unique and valuable–and they will likely grow in value as time marches on.

We're never going to have the opportunity to sit down with our grandkids or adult children and share with them the full extent of our experiences with adversity and the insights we've gained—at least as much as we would like. In fact, we may not even be around to meet some of our grandkids or great-grandkids. Maybe it's time to take a few less pictures and start writing down more lessons.

As we were writing this chapter, we mused about how photographs of people adorn our walls at home, and how cool it would be if those same people framed meaningful journal entries on how they became better by overcoming some of life's many mountains. Journals may only be blue or black ink on white paper, but they add more color than any photo could.

Writing tracks your progress. Reading your past writings is of tremendous benefit because it allows you to validate your progress and accomplishments. Retirement is a time span when you'll question your effectiveness and purpose, so having the ability to reflect over the past year can really encourage you that you *are* doing good things, even when it doesn't feel like it.

Reading your entries brings your objective voice into play and helps you recognize what was truly problematic, or what was just "noise" in your life that could have been neutralized. It's amazing how the simple act of journaling can become a self-soothing practice to refresh your outlook and mental state of being. It creates an opportunity to assess the state of your affairs from a bird's-eye view rather than allowing a reactionary life to rule the day.

Both of us value this process even though we're not yet retired. For retirees, it's even more critical, because they are no longer surrounded by the structure that more naturally led to measurable progress.

What Should a Journal Entry Look Like?

There's no exact blueprint for making a journal entry. We both have been journaling consistently for years and have a different approach, yet we each have seen tremendous benefits from the discipline. You'll eventually arrive at what works best for you, but if you need a few suggestions for starters, read on to learn about some we've found useful over time.

Keep a yearly journal that opens with a theme.
Start a new journal each year, and open with a theme that reflects where you're at personally and where you want to head in the next 365 days. I (Joel) always like to start with something I've learned over the last few years. If my wife or kids ever open up my journal, I want them to be inspired.

> There's no exact blueprint for making a journal entry. You'll eventually arrive at what works best for you.

Next, ponder questions like the following. Pretend you're a wise old sage, and write something reflective or forward-thinking.

- Who am I as a person?
- Which loved ones and friends do I want to bring into this collection of entries?
- Do I find myself in a valley, at the summit, or somewhere on the ascent?
- What did I learn from my last journal, and to what do I aspire in this next journal?
- What are some of my goals?

Limit it to just one page, a few times a week.
When many people begin journaling, they love it. In fact, they love it too much, so they write, like, six pages. Not good. It's sort of like going to the gym on January 1. You haven't worked out in four years, but now you're a new you! So you work out for two hours … and then you're too sore to go back. In journaling, keep it to one page at a sitting, and journal only a few days per week. Many people will tout daily journaling, but we don't think that's realistic with all we have going on. Like anything, it's

good to have a day off; otherwise your entries can get boring. Adding some time in between allows life to throw a few more curveballs your way.

Don't worry about perfection. No English composition teacher is here to grade you. You're free to not form every sentence correctly. You don't even have to worry about spelling! If someone reads it years after you're gone, they'll understand that a journal is informal and personal; it wasn't made to be published (unless you become famous). Meanwhile, it feels good to put something down that doesn't have to be perfect. This is just you and any lesson, feeling, or observation you would like to get onto the page. Big sigh.

Include three ingredients. From rereading past journal entries, you'll begin to identify what structure and themes are most useful to you. Here are some we have noticed:

1. **Something light:** A brief bit about a positive thing you've experienced, such as a trip or a memorable moment with a loved one or colleague. It might be as simple as noting you had a great weekend and why. Try to incorporate some informative details as you unpack your activities.

   For example, when journaling about a recent family vacation at the beach, I (Joel) could have simply said, "We went to the beach and built a sandcastle together." But what I actually wrote took on a larger meaning:

   > It was 72 degrees today, just warm enough to make a dip in the cold water refreshing

and the breeze unnoticeable. Ethan [my second oldest] jumped right in and started constructing the same sandcastle I had built the day before, with little help from him. It brought a smile to my face to watch him jump right in and try without Dad's help. Owen [my oldest son], who is all about soccer and thinks he dislikes art, jumped right in alongside Ethan and had the cool and creative idea to add seashells to the castle. It was great to see him doing something imaginative as opposed to juggling a ball!

Hopefully you can see how I told a light story but incorporated some useful details and traits to paint a better picture of who my kids are.

2. **Something meaty:** Take a paragraph and go deeper into something you've learned or you're reflecting on. For me, I like to weave in my spiritual walk and document how I'm growing, what I'm learning, and what I'm struggling with. Sometimes I write about things that life happens to be teaching me as I age. These lessons can be very valuable for you as you reread.

3. **Something for someone else:** This is certainly optional, but we like to specifically pick certain events or discussions with our children, spouse, parents, or other loved ones that give us reason to smile when we read about them again. And if your family

picks up your journal one day, it will be like they are having a treasured conversation with you.

I (Alex) keep a journal specifically to give to my children when they are adults. Keeping a separate journal for others isn't something you need to feel compelled to do—I just personally prefer to have one written directly to my children. It starts just prior to our eldest child's birth. The journal offers a clear glimpse into precious memories that surely would have been lost to time.

I stay committed to writing entries that will hopefully help them with life perspective when they're older—and so they can have a true glimpse of themselves and our family during their formative years. And selfishly, it's something that brings me immense joy to revisit. Here is the first entry I wrote in the weeks leading up to our first child being born—a time when I was facing a healthy dose of uncertainty:

> To my unborn children.
>
> Right now, I'm sitting quietly in a coffee shop, looking out a black pane window. I have the longest run of my life tomorrow, a 50k trail run that has a daunting 6,000 feet of gain. Despite training for the last 5 months, I feel unprepared. There is much uncertainty ahead and definitely some fear. But when you strive to achieve something bold, there's

always underlying stress. Without it, you know you aren't aiming high enough. If there's no chance of failure, then there's no real chance of success. The clock ticks toward the start of my race; obviously the race itself is a trifle—it's an arbitrary distance and event, but I think the process and emotions underlying it fit the same mold that anything else boundary-pushing produces.

Accomplishment of something bigger than yourself, physically or otherwise, can be such a fulfilling process. A person is a small speck in the universe, but that doesn't mean we aren't destined for something great and meaningful. Time is finite, but what you do is written in permanence forever, so make sure you are happy about the paths you choose.

As I run for probably 7+ hours tomorrow, intentionally breaking myself down on a dusty trail, my mind will be on you. When I approach the finish and see your mom and her bump, it will be the most beautiful thing I've ever seen in my life. Can't wait, love you.

Dad

Think if you had a compilation of raw memories like this one to revisit later in life. All your entries won't be earth shattering revelations; some will simply be cherished memories that would have otherwise been forgotten, and others offer meaningful perspective and life context. The point is, journaling can help more than just you. It's an incredible gift you can use to encourage others. Not that you need to hand your granddaughter your journal, but if she happens to be dealing with a life challenge, you may be able to draw upon past entries to help her in a one-on-one conversation. The benefits can be far reaching if you take the time to put pen to paper now.

Finish each journal with reflection. Have you ever noticed that a whole year can go by, and yet you don't feel like you've accomplished much? Sure, you may be able to remember the big events. But were there fractional improvements along the way? A summary on the final pages of your journal can make this much clearer. Journaling is the counterweight to momentary musings of *What difference am I making? Other people are accomplishing so many things, but I'm not.*

> Journaling can help more than just you. It's an incredible gift you can use to encourage others.

I (Joel) will admit, this ending activity can take a bit of time (about four weeks in my case). I have to reread my journal, and as I do so, I jot down on a notepad things that jump out at me. I categorize them by "Family," "Work," "Travel," "Personal Growth," "Challenges I've Overcome," and so forth.

I can tell you that there hasn't been a single year when I wasn't shocked by how much more was accomplished than what I had assumed or "felt." Thankfully, feelings don't beat hard cold facts. When you condense these items to four or five pages, it's powerful—they are like "encouragement concentrate."

It's certainly a good reminder that you're doing more good than you think—a great remedy for your negative bias—but also, whenever you find yourself in a rut (and you will), you can simply pull out your journal from any year, read your summary, and become encouraged.

This is one of the primary benefits of journaling: It can help vault you out of any holes you might find yourself in. But once you're back on the ground, don't stop. Keep writing.

For whatever reason, this chapter's topic garners the most comments ... both good and bad. We wanted to close Key 4 with some insight from one of our readers, Wilton Rivera of Seattle, Washington.

> One of the big takeaways I had in reading *Afterwork* is the chapter on journaling. Why journal? Create a diary? Seems a little effeminate for me. However, I thought I would try it a bit. Why not? If I didn't like it, I could always stop, right? After a week of "making an effort" to do this at the end of each day, it was actually an eye-opener. I was rewarded by, number one: Reminders of the little victories, the good things that happened to me on those days. Being a pessimist, I tend to hone in and focus on the negatives and sometimes forget the positives during the day. Journaling allowed me to revisit those "good times," those "feel good"

moments. Number two: It felt good writing. There is something about putting your thoughts on paper. The initial intention of just writing a few snippets/sentences has now morphed into multiple paragraphs. I now find myself writing on the plane when I go on trips (both on business and pleasure) and in hotel rooms. Who knew?[35]

Key 5: Faith

Do you know who John Tyler was? If that name doesn't sound familiar, then surely you know who Benjamin Harrison was. No?

Actually, both of these gentlemen were presidents of the United States—Tyler was the tenth and Harrison the twenty-third. Maybe this goes to show that 99 percent of us won't be remembered into the distant future either. I mean, if presidents get forgotten, the prognosis isn't great. As the ancient King David wrote, "Our days on earth are like grass; like wildflowers, we bloom and die. The wind blows, and we are gone—as though we had never been here."[36]

If we camp on this thought for any length of time, it feels pretty discouraging. Why attempt to make our last few decades great if the fun simply ends when we do? All the effort we put into making our mark, searching for meaning and seeking to leave a legacy, even serving others unselfishly … and most of it won't be remembered?

This would be a good time to ask ourselves, *What is it inside of us that even wants to be remembered? And why does it disappoint us that we may eventually be forgotten, failing to leave an impactful legacy that people will talk about for years to come?* One possible answer to the first question is pride, and perhaps the answer to the second is our need to feel significant.

Yet if our names and deeds will likely fade to gray at the end of retirement, what are we striving for? What drives our value system, especially if we've moved out from behind the facade of a corporate structure? Why do we care about being good, or choosing right over wrong? Why does it still feel good to help someone?

> Left to our own devices, we tend to wreak havoc on our own lives and those around us.

We can tell you one thing: By ourselves, in our own strength, we're incapable of ensuring a wonderful *afterwork* that catapults us into something far greater than we've known. Human nature has not simply evolved toward that kind of inherent power or goodness. You don't have to be around many people very long to learn that we can be pretty messed up. Left to our own devices, we tend to wreak havoc on our own lives and those around us. This is one of the primary reasons for bulging Alcoholics Anonymous groups, high levels of depression, an American divorce every thirty-six *seconds*,[37] mass shootings, a drug epidemic, and quieter issues such as feeling unfulfilled or unhappy. The list goes on—and we've done it to ourselves.

Our Internal Division

Psychology and faith share one fundamental agreement: Internal division—an inner void characterized by discontentment and a lack of peace—leads to chaos and destruction. Of course, knowing this strife exists, and knowing how to find alignment, are two very different things. There's a helpful and transformational way to fill the void, and there's a way that actually makes the problem worse, even if it leads to temporary "fun."

Elizabeth Gilbert, popular journalist and author of *Eat, Pray, Love,* theorizes that "somewhere within us all, there does exist a supreme Self who is eternally at peace."[38] But read on, and you may find her observation rather ironic. She got very honest in a 2015 article for the *New York Times* entitled "Confessions of a Seduction Addict":

> I careened from one intimate entanglement to the next—dozens of them—without so much as a day off between romances. Seduction was never a casual sport for me; it was more like a heist, adrenalizing and urgent. I would plan the heist for months, scouting out the target, looking for unguarded entries. Then I would break into his deepest vault, steal all his emotional currency and spend it on myself.
>
> I might indeed win the man eventually. But over time (and it wouldn't take long), his unquenchable infatuation for me would fade, as his attention returned to everyday matters. This always left me feeling abandoned and invisible; love that could be quenched was not nearly enough love for me.[39]

Does it sound like she found that eternally peaceful supreme self? We are not making light of her divided outlook and actions; we all have our own versions of such behavior. But it draws out the fact that this world is not going to help any of us solve the problem. It will only compound it, as was the case for Elizabeth Gilbert. With each striving came a greater thirst.

Let us make a bold statement here: We believe this humanly unbridgeable gap we're calling "division" is hardwired by God. It is a need and a thirst for something greater that we cannot quench alone. We are at best an "unfinished" project, consisting of a void unfillable by stuff, activities, and efforts. It's as fundamental as the reality of right and wrong, gravity, and the sun continuing to rise.

There are many acceptable vices we use to try to assimilate happiness and peace into our internal discontentment. They can be anything from shopping too much, distracting ourselves with certain hobbies, pouring ourselves into work, overly focusing on our children or grandchildren, placing an exaggerated emphasis on fitness, or overeating.

These don't jump off the page as unhealthy, but for that very reason they can in some ways be worse. It's easier to justify something to yourself when it's socially acceptable, making you less aware there's an issue in the first place.

But there are also darker vices, such as alcohol and substance abuse, physical and emotional affairs, lust, perhaps a desire at retirement age to "try something new with someone else." Teresa Collett, professor of law at the University of St. Thomas, wrote about the growing "gray divorce revolution," a phenomenon we mentioned earlier:

> We live in a time where divorce is both common and socially acceptable. And while **general divorce rates are declining**, for those age 50 and above divorce rates have doubled since 1990. **For those age 65 and above the rates have tripled.**

Collett goes on to acknowledge the harm done and then reveals the primary cause:

> Gray divorce is more than a personal loss—it hurts families, friends, and communities. It is time for us to say so in our words and our actions. No one should stay in an unsafe relationship, but abuse is the cause of only a comparatively small proportion of divorces. **Far more common are divorces due to discontent—with our self, our spouse, or life in general.**[40]

It doesn't matter how much water you pour into a bucket if there's a hole in the bottom.

We have personally witnessed many retiree divorces that took place after almost a lifetime of marriage. The reasons varied, but all were manifestations of trying to bridge the gap of internal division.

Retirement brings a unique and potent combination: a shorter timeline coupled with more free time. It gives that inner voice of division a louder voice. *FEED ME, BECAUSE TIME'S ALMOST UP!* it shouts.

Internal division is a problem we instinctively want to fix. We are constantly trying to plug the hole or fill the gap or build a bridge to peace, to fulfillment. Yet it doesn't matter how much water you pour into a bucket if there's a hole in the bottom.

We've seen some of the most well-intentioned, seemingly balanced people succumb to this illusion. The sad part is that we know from experience how the story ends: badly, and with plenty of regret—or perhaps even worse.

It's a misconception that young adults are the most prone to suicide. Recent statistics show that "younger groups have had consistently lower suicide rates than middle-aged and older adults."[41] There's a darkness that comes when you realize you've made a mistake and are running out of time to fix it.

Each of us would no doubt say, "I want the best for myself." Very well; we're not saying you shouldn't have fun and experience life's deep treasures as you pursue a better version of yourself. But the truth is that if you make yourself into a god and go on chasing only your own desires, life doesn't turn out very good. The result is emptiness.

Faith Helps Bridge the Divide

So where, you may ask, does faith fit into this picture of inner division?

For one thing, faith removes the prideful stance of "It's all about me" and puts us in our proper place within the world, posturing us to enjoy a more meaningful and impactful life.

It also allows us to sense that we are wonderfully created. When we stop to think about all the parts and pieces that need to work together every day just to keep our bodies alive, we realize how truly remarkable our existence is.

Faith bridges our inner divide and connects us to our Creator and his personal design for each one of us—a design that promises a bright future beyond the bounds of this world.

Some also see a life of faith as laying down one's will in exchange for something better, and in some ways that is true. It's not such a bad deal if surrendering our pride and recognizing our place in the world can actually lead us toward a greater story.

Living with faith—accepting that you can't explain everything and that something bigger than us created all that we see—brings a better result in your own life and in the lives of those you associate with each day. Granted, doing so requires a degree of trust. You must be vulnerable enough to let your guard down and take this premise "on faith," so to speak. But faith is truly remarkable for those who earnestly pursue it.

A definition in the Bible says that "faith is the substance of things hoped for, the evidence of things not seen."[42] You may find it odd to hear the words *faith* and *substance* used in the same sentence. After all, substance is tangible, whereas faith in God, believing in the afterlife, and attempting to follow the path God has laid before us are all, of course, intangible. But the effect on our lives is quite real and recognizable. The *substance* is in the growth and outcome that results from living out one's faith.

> Living with faith brings a better result in your own life and in the lives of those you associate with each day.

We don't say this lightly or superficially, as if trying to convert someone to our personal beliefs. It is rather an earnest description of what we have seen firsthand in our own lives as parents, husbands, brothers, and of course, financial planners.

Having faith in God, we acknowledge the brevity of life with the understanding that we are meaningful but so small in comparison to God. We recognize that we indeed are not masters of the universe—by design we can't be! We must set aside our pride, ask for forgiveness, thank God for what he has given, perhaps even kneel or bow our heads or clasp our hands (in gestures of servitude and yielding) to pray. In that process, we not only set aside silly underpinnings that permeate our society but also take a step toward overcoming our inner division and identifying what fulfills us.

Living Today in Light of Tomorrow

Erwin McManus, an accomplished author and pastor, tells a story in his book *The Last Arrow* that helps explain how the life beyond this one impacts us today. He was attending a conference in Mysore, India, alongside Devdutt Pattanaik, an Indian physician who calls himself a "mythologist." He elaborates,

> I was most struck by [Pattanaik's] humorous and insightful contrast between Eastern and Western thought. His focus was on how the different myths that shape our worldviews affect us when we attempt to engage in business. But the implications go far beyond that. He contrasted the Indian mind-set, which approaches life more naturally with fuzzy logic, fluidity, and contextualization, with the Western mind-set, which is more prone toward facts, logic, and standardization. He pointed out that Hindus believing in reincarnation are not in a hurry, as they believe they have many lives to get things done, which is in contrast to the ancient Greeks,

who believed that each person had only one life and, because of this, had a greater sense of urgency.... Pattanaik wasn't advocating the rightness of either view; he was simply stating a fact that how we view our existence has a radical effect on our engagement in this life.[43]

Erwin pondered what he was hearing and then proceeded to provide some of his own insight:

Although there is much I admire about Eastern thought, I prefer the effect of what Pattanaik would call Western mythology.... I am absolutely convinced that what we do in this life matters and that time is our most precious commodity.... There are no trial runs. In that sense, life does not allot us do-overs....

Seeing the contrast between these two worldviews helps me understand the power of the Hebraic mind-set. At the intersection of Western and Eastern worldviews, the Hebrews were compelled by both the one and the infinite. We each have one life, but this life has eternal significance. What we do in this one life has infinite implications, and beyond that, our stories are bigger than history. Our stories don't end when we do. They are only the beginning of much greater stories, the content of which we are completely unaware. So in that sense we get the best of both worlds. Our deepest meaning must go beyond that which is confined to time and space, yet that does not in any way diminish the importance of this moment. If the urgency of one life is what compels us to live our most heroic lives, then let's make the most of this one life each of us has. At the same time, we can only live that most heroic life well when we have a deep sense of connectedness to that which is infinite and eternal.[44]

Faith: A New Kind of Habit

Being connected to something beyond ourselves can break the dastardly chains that confine our sense of purpose and meaning to only this life. You are not here just passing time until someone turns the light switch off, striving to make sure you're remembered. You have a purpose beyond yourself, but also a significant purpose within yourself.

> Faith is a habit with an incredible power to shape our lives.

Faith is a habit with an incredible power to shape our lives. Does it sound strange to describe faith as a habit? C. S. Lewis, the Irish-born scholar who tried to prove his atheism and eventually convinced himself that God exists, said that we "must train the habit of Faith."[45] One commentator went on to explain,

His point is a good one. All of us are caught every day inside the shifting moods of our emotions. If our schedule is thwarted by a slight rearrangement, our health fails us, our food digests badly, or the weather strikes as humid or foggy or simmering, we might begin to doubt everything. "This rebellion of your moods against your real self is going to come anyway.... We have to be continually reminded of what we believe," says Lewis. "Neither this belief nor any other will automatically remain alive in the mind. It must be fed."[46]

So, what's your belief system? At this stage of life, are you still feeding it? Like any other habit, discipline, or state of mind discussed in this book, it doesn't grow on its own. And if it doesn't grow, it's not going to make the impact you need.

Without faith, life can be void of an ultimate life-purpose; it becomes an elusive, time-wasting struggle to find lasting fulfillment in the wrong places. Knowing that time is fleeting and the sand in our hourglass has almost trickled to the bottom, we are caught in an internal struggle to handle the reality of *It's almost over* and *I haven't found it yet.* So we move on to the next thing, hoping for a better result. But how sweet it is when we know the last drop of sand in that hourglass is but a release into something beyond our wildest dreams.

Challenges and Rewards in the Journey Ahead

Now of course, a life of faith is always worth it, but it isn't always easy. You don't arrive at faith and launch every day with a wonderful feeling inside. It doesn't help you explain why a loved one may suffer or your kids and grandkids may struggle. It doesn't fit in a perfect little box where life is just lovely.

Don't be surprised if your faith journey isn't perfect. Bad things will still happen. Good things will also happen. We live in a terrible and beautiful world, the complexities of which simply cannot be explained until the day when we meet God face-to-face.

One writer who experienced both the good and the terrible in his own life had much to say about living a life of faith. Originally called Saul of Tarsus, he was a Jewish leader who was strong on religion—and void of faith. He knew what to say and what to eat and what not to do. He even ordered the imprisonment and murder of many who followed a revolutionary leader named Jesus. But God caught Saul's attention with a series of miracles. He blinded Saul as he was walking one day, then spoke to him and gave him a mission that was strong on faith and void of religion. (There's more to the story if you care to read it in the Book of Acts.)

Saul stopped worshiping his religious practices, flipped the script, and turned to a life of faith. In fact, he went on to preach faith throughout the Mediterranean world, now known by his Roman name—the apostle Paul. He was also the second most prolific contributor to the writings of the New Testament, the portion of the Bible where grace and mercy reign. Talk about an about-face!

Paul's biography demonstrates that we can all change. We don't have to be a victim of our past, which for many of us has already stolen so much. Our past doesn't get to have a say in our future if we don't want it to. Faith gives us the courage to change and the confidence to know it will make a difference.

Now hear Paul's inspiring piece regarding faith in action:

> Let love be genuine. Abhor what is evil; hold fast to what is good. Love one another with brotherly affection. Outdo one another in showing honor. Do not be slothful in zeal, be fervent in spirit,

serve the Lord. Rejoice in hope, be patient in tribulation, be constant in prayer. Contribute to the needs of the saints and seek to show hospitality.

Bless those who persecute you; bless and do not curse them. Rejoice with those who rejoice, weep with those who weep. Live in harmony with one another. Do not be haughty, but associate with the lowly. Never be wise in your own sight. Repay no one evil for evil, but give thought to do what is honorable in the sight of all. If possible, so far as it depends on you, live peaceably with all. Beloved, never avenge yourselves, but leave it to the wrath of God, for it is written, "Vengeance is mine, I will repay, says the Lord." ... Do not be overcome by evil, but overcome evil with good.[47]

> We don't have to be a victim of our past, which for many of us has already stolen so much. Faith gives us the courage to change and the confidence to know it will make a difference.

Can any of us think of a better set of values to anchor the post-career years? Probably not. If we simply do what is written here, we will surely find fulfillment.

Jumping ahead twenty centuries, we'll leave you with one of the most famous movie quotes of all time, spoken by Andy Dufresne in *The Shawshank Redemption*: "I guess it comes down to a simple choice, really. Get busy living or get busy dying."

Key 6: Connection

All through your years in the workplace, you probably had plenty of company (sometimes more than you wanted, right?!) because you joined (or created) an organization and forged professional and personal relationships with those on every side. You couldn't help interacting with others in a never-ending inflow. Maybe you even spent more time with some of those people than you did with your own spouse.

If you were also raising children, you interacted with them, their friends, their friends' parents, their teachers, their coaches, and others in the community. During those decades of life, connections were prefabricated. You simply plugged into certain microcommunities without even trying.

But now you've left the workforce. The children have grown up and moved away. You wake up in a quiet house every morning to face another quiet day, because life's new structure no longer provides daily opportunities to connect. You're not getting that constant supply of new relationships that, in reality, offered nurture without your knowing it.

Maintaining a level of connection with others is now a burden you must take upon yourself. You can no longer consider it automatic. Your tight-knit, long-term connections haven't been lost, but instead of passively riding the community train that once moved them forward on predetermined tracks, you're now traveling in an off-road 4x4. This very different, bumpy-riding vehicle has the ability to take you along new and scenic routes, but you must choose to steer in those directions.

What the Research Shows

It's not surprising that studies have proven loneliness is prevalent among retirees. So is anxiety and depression. And what if we told you that loneliness is as dangerous to your longevity as smoking fifteen cigarettes a day? Or that loneliness is even *more* dangerous than obesity?

Well, it's true, according to a 2018 wide-ranging study by Cigna, the health insurance giant.[48] An earlier report by Dr. Julianne Holt-Lunstad provided a similar conclusion. She analyzed nearly 150 studies that included about three hundred thousand people. The data found that "people with strong social bonds are 50 percent less likely to die over a given period of time than those who have fewer social connections."[49]

We all know that inhaling chemical-laced smoke into our lungs is awful for our health; this is indisputable. What's not immediately obvious is the severely negative mental *and* physical health effects triggered by a lack of connection to others.

Quality over Quantity

So what combats depression fueled by loneliness? It is in fact not the *quantity* of relationships but the *quality*. The depth of your relationships is what truly matters, not the latitude of your social web. Even if you are a socialite, constantly showing up at parties and community activities, there will be little benefit if your relationships are superficial. The quality of our relationships is something we can directly control. We all need to work toward meaningful interactions—starting with our loved ones.

As the two of us work with hundreds of *afterwork* households regarding their financial arrangements, it's amazing how often we hear about conflicts that have nothing to do with money. Husbands and wives are clashing when suddenly they're both at home. The two lovebirds who previously led loosely separate lives during the workweek are now constantly at odds.

In many cases it started right after the initial "sugar rush." Soon one or even both individuals reverted back to what they knew—getting another job similar to what they had previously. They did

> The depth of your relationships is what truly matters, not the latitude of your social web.

this simply to "get out of the house" and chase the old purposeful connections they felt comfortable with, even though it meant just treading water in their lives. Sometimes the result was another "gray divorce," which we discussed in the previous chapter.

Remember the old Johnny Lee song that won a Grammy Award, "Looking for Love in All the Wrong Places"? Well, these divorces were cases of looking for *purpose* in all the wrong places. They didn't *not* love their spouse; after all, they'd been married for forty years or more. They just didn't fill the hole— their inner division—with the right things.

Are you noticing a pattern here? If *movement* is your physical therapy (Key 3) and *journaling* is your counselor (Key 4), *connection* is your safety net. The number one push to move in the wrong direction in life relationships begins with isolation. Each example we have witnessed and could describe had one person who withdrew and began escaping, leaving friends, church, and so forth. Isolation is your enemy.

If you find yourself doing retirement solo, you have an entirely unique set of challenges to consider. No one is there to converse with you or share the day's hardship or victories. In some ways this can be easier than dealing with a stressful, tense relationship ... see above. But you are still more susceptible to loneliness and the problems that come with it.

Whatever the setting or circumstances, you must go against your own inertia and simply force yourself into situations that will bring about connection over time. Which relationships in your life have you neglected during your "busy" years? Which "close friends" have you actually not seen for a long time, even though they're just a phone call away? What relatives have you always wished to get to know better if your schedule wasn't so packed with X, Y, and Z? Now is the time to ponder the quality of those relationships and start making an effort.

> "If you want to go fast, go alone. If you want to go far, go together." –African proverb

Like most habits in this book, at first it will feel like work. After all, who really wants to get up early for a coffee date, or rally to prepare dinner with a group of friends on a lazy Sunday afternoon? But keep in mind you'll always be thankful that as time goes by and the relationships you've invested in deepen, the returns begin to compound into greater benefits. You'll find yourself less bored and more fulfilled as you enjoy outlets for having fun as well as sharing your deeper, more personal emotions. The

African proverb says it well: "If you want to go fast, go alone. If you want to go far, go together."

Connecting with Others through Serving

As we have mentioned previously, this life stage is unique in that you are at a maximum point of experience and have more time and presumably more financial resources than ever before. This potent combination equates to an enormous level of flexibility and impact.

Don't underestimate the vast amount of energy and talent within you just waiting to serve something much larger than yourself. In physics we learn about *potential energy* (imagine a ball being held above the ground) and *kinetic energy* (the ball flying through the air, energy in motion). We just need to turn our potential energy into kinetic energy— and we can do that almost exclusively through our connection with others.

Think of the individuals, families, and organizations you associate with. Is there a specific way you can leverage your unique abilities and resources to impact them? Perhaps you could become a mentor, or channel specific knowledge from your career in a way that transforms an organization and connects you with the people they serve.

Connecting through serving certainly beats squandering your days on social media and web-surfing. In fact, current research attributes loneliness to time spent staring at a screen and perusing social media. Most people post only the best snapshots of their lives to meet that unquenchable societal standard of "perfect." It's a self-defeating cycle, like materialism ("I need more stuff") or evaluating yourself strictly on performance ("I'll never be good enough"). This kind of self-talk eventually punctures our self-worth.

Coping with Lost Connections

Loss comes in many types, and we don't want to minimize any of them. You may be grieving the end of your career, or perhaps you were forced to retire earlier than planned. Maybe you've lost a longtime furry companion and it feels like saying goodbye to a family member. You may have been financially secure, but then something happened to bring that into question. Perhaps someone close to you has experienced a permanent life-altering health event. And the list goes on.

Engaging in an online community does not always equate to meaningful connection.

During your *afterwork* years, more than at any other time in your life, you're also likely to endure the loss of a dear loved one—an experience so difficult that it could lead you to stop living out your purpose.

Facing this last season of life without your loved one wasn't in your script. You had a plan—and it was taken from you. "Unfair" doesn't even begin to scratch the surface.

Nobody can provide the right insight to ease your pain. Only time and grieving will achieve that. But we want to share some things you can do to help.

What follows isn't meant to be an exhaustive list,

but we hope it somewhat helps to prepare you if something bad does happen, or helps you change the way you're dealing with a loss that's already occurred.

1. Make Financial Preparations

We've been honored to walk alongside clients who've endured such a loss, either suddenly or gradually. Whatever the timing, it's wise to already be working with a financial professional, because the weight of dealing with a loss while simultaneously trying to relearn your entire financial existence is too great to bear.

If you happen to be a couple, know that it's common for one spouse to take a back seat when it comes to dealing with finances. Not ideal. Even if you or your spouse isn't heavily involved in the day-to-day, it's a good practice to take the initiative by attending meetings with your advisor and asking questions. You'll find the cursory understanding is very helpful whenever the unforeseen occurs. If you haven't been engaged in those conversations, it's time to get involved.

2. Invest in Your Physical Care

Now more than ever is the time to take care of yourself physically. You will feel lost in your grief at times; this is part of the process to reach a reasonable level of healing. But if you let go of all the things in your life that resemble "normal," you'll be in a worse spot.

You may say you don't have the strength to take care of yourself ... or the desire, for that matter. But it's at this point that your normal disciplines can make an even bigger difference—even those as simple as making your bed, getting some movement in, eating breakfast, and taking a warm shower. These little steps will help you retain a sense of self-accomplishment and momentum.

3. Seek Meaningful Connections

A third point: You may not feel excited to engage in connection with others. We get it; you want to be alone. But turning outward for support and comfort is critical. Lean on friends, family, perhaps your local church, or a support group you've built over the years. You'll find that being in relationship encourages openness and promotes healing.

Also, please know that seeking a professional counselor is not a sign of weakness. In fact, even if you aren't dealing with a loss but find yourself in any tough spot, we encourage you to seek professional help. We've heard from those who have, and there's no regret—only thankfulness for what this humble step helped achieve.

4. Practice Gratitude

We previously mentioned gratitude as a way to seek out your purpose (Key 1). Reflecting on what you're grateful for is a simple way to identify areas of your life that you inherently value. Gratitude can also help you see your loss in a larger context. It allows you to acknowledge your pain while continuing to see the good in your existence and the truth that your life is not completely derailed, despite how it may feel in the moment. It can give you courage in those dark depths to draw closer to what (and who) you are thankful for and blessed by, shining light on just how fortunate you may be, despite crushing grief.

5. Lean into Faith

You might also be surprised to hear that engaging your faith *honestly* can bring incredible healing. The Bible offers many examples of heroes of the faith who were bluntly honest with God about the way they felt.

King David wrote in Psalm 22, "God, God … my God! Why did you dump me miles from nowhere? Doubled up with pain, I call to God all the day long. No answer. Nothing. I keep at it all night, tossing and turning"[50]

But in the very next psalm—one that many of us know well—David wrote, "Even when the way goes through Death Valley, I'm not afraid when you walk by my side. Your trusty shepherd's crook makes me feel secure."[51]

We can't find peace if we're looking to understand everything that happens in this life. But it can still be healing to be honest with God. We have nothing to hide, and he can take it. If we lean into our faith with an open honesty, we're likely to find the burden is a little lighter.

Healing from the loss of meaningful connections has no shortcuts. As you keep putting one foot in front of the other, the thick clouds will gradually scatter, and blue skies will reappear. This doesn't replace what could have been, but you can enter into something new and beautiful if you're willing to fight for it.

Key 7: Learning

At the very beginning of this book, we talked about how vacations need a counterbalance to serve their intended purpose. We said that if your whole life's a vacation, then you don't have true vacations anymore. It's a self-defeating cycle—similar to our concept of the occasional lazy morning, which can occur only in the context of "not-lazy mornings."

If the *afterwork* season of your life isn't properly planned, the most common result will be to run out in search of part-time or full-time employment. That's the "easy button," so to speak. Just get hired somewhere, and you'll get back to a schedule, a reason to get up, people to interact with, a paycheck (whether you need it or not), a sense of seasonality and texture in your life, vacation time, a recognized role in a larger strategy or objective … you'll feel useful again.

There *is* a more fulfilling route, but it's harder.

Learning is actually the best surrogate to reentering the labor force in search of something fulfilling. The word *surrogate* is Latin in origin and means "to choose in place of another," or "substitute."[52] It's a piece of the counterbalancing puzzle you're trying to assemble. The Renaissance theologian and philosopher Erasmus set the stage nicely when he said, "Live as if you are to die tomorrow; study as if you were to live forever."[53]

If learning is pursued meaningfully, it has the power to improve other areas of your life without much additional effort. For example, imagine a woman who has always wanted to help couples who are struggling in their marriages. She derived great benefit from time she spent with her own counselor many years prior, and she always thought she would be good at providing the same services. But she just hasn't had time during her working years to ramp up her education in pursuit of a desire that pays next to nothing.

After retiring, she decides that taking some formal counseling classes would be fun and challenging while equipping her with the necessary tools. She enrolls at a local college and is pleased to meet a few other "more mature" students on campus; after all, learning isn't just a young person's game anymore.

> If learning is pursued meaningfully, it has the power to improve other areas of your life without much additional effort.

She thoroughly enjoys the courses, because as it turns out, learning is a lot more fun when you don't *have to* do it. After two years of study, she is formally licensed as a marriage and family counselor. She accepts a volunteer role at a local nonprofit that provides these services for free to a struggling demographic. Yes, that's correct—she *paid* for an education that she turned around and is giving away for free. (That's what you call a "purpose.")

Here are some of the collateral benefits that learning has brought to her life:

- She enjoyed the rigors of the schooling challenge; she liked being tested. She also enjoyed the seasons off (Thanksgiving, Christmas, spring break, summertime). Her calendar had texture.

- She forged meaningful new relationships with people she was able to study and work alongside.

- She was surprised at how much she enjoyed speaking into the lives of younger students in the group portions of their classes.

- She enjoyed the victory that came with accomplishing a goal.

- She loves putting her newfound knowledge into practice by helping others.

- She receives tremendous fulfillment from the concept of "doing this for free" because she wants to give back.

- She now gets to enjoy vacations as much as she did during her career, because every day isn't a vacation!

- She has lots of good stories to journal about and revisit later in life as she reflects on her legacy.

- She is incredibly thankful she didn't forgo this opportunity in exchange for the easy answer of going back to a paying job.

We could keep going … but it all started with learning.

Uncharted Territory

Maybe you don't have a personal wish like this to draw upon. No problem—just pick something that has always interested you and start learning about it. Trust that the purpose will unfold even if you don't have a master plan. Learning is as much about the journey as the destination.

In our roles as financial advisors, we've found that people generally hesitate to try new things. They tend to stick to the way they've always lived. Many have a vague sense of something they would like to try but don't really know where to start or how they will ultimately use the tools they acquire. If they can't foresee the final result from the beginning, they don't want to step out and make the attempt.

> Learning is as much about the journey as the destination.

All of this is perfectly understandable, but if they can shift their perspectives and realize that learning is an adventure, it can take them places they weren't expecting to go. As the Greek philosopher Plutarch said, "The correct analogy for the mind is not a vessel that needs filling, but wood that needs igniting."[54]

When you step away from the structure that has been your life for years upon years, it's time for something new and exciting. It's time to gain knowledge you can offer to a world in need of innovation and goodwill. If you're still passionate about what you did in your career and feel it gave you skills that can still make an impact, by all means use them—but try drawing upon those old reserves in a new way.

If you're a physician, why not take some time to volunteer with Doctors Without Borders in a developing country? If you're an engineer, could you lend your expertise to a nonprofit that is serving an unfamiliar demographic? If you're a financial advisor, why not look for ways to educate the aspiring younger generation who knows little about finance and its importance for a proper start in life?

Learning and adventuring toward new horizons in retirement is such an exciting proposition. The two of us have observed many of our clients undertaking entirely new endeavors and loving the purpose and fulfillment they bring. But remember: There still might be more to learn within the same vein that you're accustomed to. Don't fall into the trap of thinking you need to undertake some new, obscure, thrill-seeking hobby if that's not what you're about.

Learning Keeps Your Mind Healthy

A recurring theme throughout this book is the idea that great things can unfold when you remove yourself from what is comfortable. Just as a physically active lifestyle keeps your body fit, there is plenty of evidence that learning keeps your mind young and healthy.

Researchers from the University of Texas at Dallas took 221 adults, ages 60–90, and separated them into three distinct groups. Each group was tasked to do fifteen hours of mental activity each week over the course of three months.

The first group had to undertake pursuits they had never attempted—quilting or digital photography. The second group was assigned familiar at-home activities such as word puzzles or listening to classical music. The third group spent their fifteen hours each week in social activities like field trips and entertainment outings.

The researchers found that only the first group— the ones challenged with new activities that required them to learn—showed clear cognitive improvement, especially in the area of memory.[55]

Learning specific new skills, tasks, and information is what helps you stay mentally young and sharp; it is not enough to simply be stimulated or engaged in an activity.

Earning Your Learning

To begin your learning quest, start by asking yourself, *What am I genuinely curious about?* We are all so different, so don't try to conform to what society labels as interesting or what your retired peers are doing.

> To begin your learning quest, start by asking yourself, *What am I genuinely curious about?*

People who explore some niche idea or unique undertaking purely out of curiosity and a desire to learn experience genuine fulfillment. It's always evident when they're passionate about something because they speak about it with excitement and fascination.

What makes *you* say, "Wow, that's amazing!" or "It would be so interesting to _____"? There literally isn't enough time to explore all the mind-blowing avenues of learning that are waiting to engage you.

It's also interesting to note that the learning process has changed drastically in the past century. Previously, someone who wanted to study a particular topic had to go to a library to find books on the subject, or they needed to correspond directly with an expert. Today, information on just about anything can instantly be found online. It's also easy to connect with groups of people who share a common interest, no matter how obscure.

This is convenient—but there is very little investment in obtaining knowledge that comes "free." You learn much less if you don't have to work at it.

For example, apps are available that translate languages in real time; you can have your own pocket translator anywhere on the planet, forgoing the need to learn another language. When my wife and I (Alex) were in Morocco, we were attempting to communicate with a taxi driver as we sped through the bumpy desert. We had cell service, though, so we were able to have a useful (and very memorable) conversation with him with each of us speaking our native tongues. This technology and its contributions to the world are remarkable, but it's unfortunate that learning and all its benefits are beginning to be bypassed.

Nonetheless, opportunities still exist to explore and enjoy any topic, if you are willing to make the effort. As Alexandre Dumas wrote in *The Count of Monte Cristo*, "I cannot think that man is meant to find happiness so easily! Happiness is like one of those palaces on an enchanted island, its gates guarded by dragons. One must fight to gain it."[56]

So get fully immersed in whatever you want to understand; delve into what triggered your curiosity in the first place. Don't settle for a Wikipedia explanation or the first hotlink that pops up. Dig beneath the surface-level information, pushing your brain to adapt to the unfamiliar. As an ancient Chinese philosopher once said, "Tell me and I forget. Teach me and I remember. Involve me and I learn."

When you get involved, you'll be amazed at what you'll gain. Remember that doing something new means that initially you may not be good at it. But as you begin to realize how much you still have to learn, you will learn a lot about yourself. Will you have the gumption to press on and seek the answers or skill required to pursue your passion? Or will the path of least resistance tempt you to stop?

If you stay focused on mastering this new endeavor because you're passionate about it, you'll feel immensely good when you reach a level of competency that you know, deep within yourself, was *earned*.

> Will you have the gumption to press on and seek the answers or skill required to pursue your passion? Or will the path of least resistance tempt you to stop?

Retirees need some wins under their belt more than anyone. You've lived too long to gain benefit from superficial praise or flattery from an outside source. Your pat on the back now comes from within. To feel accomplished, you first have to … accomplish!

On the Road Again

One couple we know, after decades in the workforce, liquidated most of their possessions (except their investment portfolio, of course), purchased a nice camper, and decided to become nomads for a year or two. They had lived in the same city for most of their careers, employed at the same companies. But now their goal was to see all of the United States, learn its history, and experience its beauty.

They began by mapping their course to hit northern national and state parks during the summer and then head south in the winter, zigzagging across the country while stopping to see family along the way. They're the kind of people who pull over at each overlook and read the entire historical sign with real curiosity.

It's approaching a decade now, and they continue this lifestyle, despite having plenty of money to stay home and be "normal retirees." Every time we speak with them on the phone (when they have cellular service, that is), it sounds something like this: "Well, we are at _____ National Park for a couple months. Bill is fly-fishing and learning how to tie his own flies. I'm volunteering at the campground site, handing out informational pamphlets about the area. I also have a new stack of books I'm eager to start."

Notice they don't have "learning" per se as an objective. They are merely following their curiosity and hearts into unknown endeavors they think they might like. Along the way (literally), they are venturing into countless new sources of learning and intrigue.

Other retirees hit two birds with one stone by blending their travel interests with grandparenting. A California couple we know has said to each grandchild, "When you're twelve years old, we'll take just you—no siblings, no parents—on a special trip all the way across the country to Washington, DC." (Notice: not Disney World or Six Flags.) "We'll explore the amazing buildings there—the White House, the monuments, the Smithsonian—learning all about our great country."

But be assured that you don't have to buy airplane tickets to enhance your knowledge. We heard about a CEO who, once his busy life in the executive suite wrapped up, decided to read a biography of *every* US president. Not just the famous ones—Washington, Jefferson, Lincoln—but also those he knew next to nothing about. How did they make decisions? What were their greatest victories? Their most crushing defeats? Did they have a faith in God to sustain them? What kind of family life did they have? This man found great enrichment through his pursuit.

Choose Your Sources Wisely

Whatever your conduit for learning—a college class, a book, a podcast, a TED Talk, a news report—we must be careful to evaluate the source. Every professor, author, speaker, and even close friend has his or her own perspective. We need to stay alert to biases and slants that influence the exchanges. Do we really want to absorb this material and embrace it as our own? Maybe it's worthy, but then again maybe it's flawed. Maybe the information is valid, but then again maybe it's a case of "spin."

The average retiree watches almost thirty-two hours of television a week.[57] And most of the channels are publicly traded corporations. These businesses have revenue targets to hit and stockholders to please. Unfortunately for you and me, good news simply doesn't sell as well as bad or shocking news. And if it doesn't sell, then the market price of advertising goes down, which hurts profitability for the company. The media bosses understand this very well; they know what will get you to watch, and that's what they air.

Our society has become so accustomed to letting movies, books, TV, and the news tell us how to feel that we almost don't know what to think apart from them. Too many times the only decision we've kept for ourselves is which side to take. We've actually joked with some of our clients about becoming wealthy by doing exactly the opposite of what the "experts" were telling them. Beware of any information outlet that has some axe to grind (which is a large majority, whether it's the TV or Facebook or your neighbor).

The other challenge, in addition to this media narrative being accepted as "normal" or "factual," is that there's not much else readily available unless you work at it a bit. As we said earlier, you have to dig deep to "earn" your learning. For example, I can easily turn my SiriusXM to Fox or CNN or NPR, but it's not as easy to dial up an awesome leadership podcast. I have to remember to download it at some point, or stream it in my car and hope my service isn't spotty. Isn't it curious that good, fulfilling content is harder to find? It's as though someone had stacked the deck against us.

We're not saying you need to bury your head in the sand and ignore world events or stop reading the newspaper. What we're hoping to convey is that you should stay keenly aware of what's intertwined with media bias. For every portion of junk, you need to add two portions of value to your intake.

The news narrative can be likened to how fast food is everywhere, but finding a wholesome meal takes effort. When you're hungry, a tasty burger and fries sounds so tempting. Go ahead and enjoy them once in a while—we certainly do—but commit yourself to other intake that will require you to search a bit. These are all your fruits and vegetables: that good podcast series, the book you need to order because your friend suggested it.

And don't hesitate to turn off the screen when you've had too much. Engaging daily with biased content while ignoring the sources that will feed you with true learning can have a similar effect on your mind that eating a burger and fries each day would have on your physical health.

> Don't let someone else's bottom line color the way you see the world or lead you to make poor decisions.

Don't let someone else's bottom line color the way you see the world or lead you to make poor decisions. After all, you can't control politics, or society, or what's going on in the Middle East or the stock market, or what happens with international trade. You can only control what you choose to do with your time. At the end of life, you're guaranteed to never say, "I wish I had spent more time absorbing bad information instead of investing in myself, my family, and my friends."

Always keep learning—from intelligent, trustworthy sources. This is a vital part of a successful and fulfilling post-career life. If you're not out there experiencing life, you're not learning. And if you're not learning, you're slowly dying from the disease called "retirement."

Key 8: Awareness

It's not difficult to observe awareness (or the lack thereof) in action on many levels. Most of us have a friend or family member who just won't stop talking, mostly about their life and their problems. We think to ourselves, *They're just so unaware!*

And we've all known someone who is just rude in general; they're not necessarily mean at heart, but they say the strangest things at the wrong time. They're clueless about their faux pas.

You may think such cases aren't that big of a deal and can simply be tolerated. You may even be guilty of the same behavior, telling yourself, *So I steal the dinner conversation with friends most of the time—they don't mind ...*

Actually, they do mind, and it does matter. If you continue to live this way, you'll find that others will start to avoid you—and this could turn into a *very* big deal.

How we carry ourselves can affect our relationships. If no one wants to be around you, that's a problem, and it's usually attributed to a lack of awareness. As Warren Buffet wrote in a 1988 letter to shareholders, "As they say in poker, 'If you've been in the game 30 minutes and you don't know who the patsy is, you're the patsy.'"[58]

I (Joel) was having coffee with my close friend Joe, and during some initial conversation he filled me in on a recent dinner he and his wife, Maddie, had endured with John and Kate, another couple they'd known for years. Both couples are retired, so they eat out together frequently. Unfortunately, over the last few years, John and Kate have been embarrassing Joe and Maddie at meals. Regardless of where they are or what they order, John and Kate always manage to complain about the food and harass the server.

Joe and Maddie, on the other hand, are the type of people who, even if dinner's not perfect, understand that the server likely has life problems just like everyone else. He or she is probably tired from working really hard and from dealing with other guests who are unaware.

Obviously the meal and service aren't bad *everywhere* this foursome goes. Lapsing into complaining mode is simply what John and Kate have allowed themselves to do. There's a kinder, more positive John and Kate inside them that could absolutely decide to change. But left unattended, they are heading down a path to isolation and miserable mindsets. Joe looked right at me as he sipped his latte and said, "We're going to give them one more try—but if it happens again, we're done."

John and Kate have a disease. They most likely take this unawareness with them into every area of life. As the apostle Paul wrote twenty centuries ago, "Don't you know that a little yeast leavens the whole batch of dough?"[59] A little unawareness can affect the whole outcome of your actions. These "not-so-big deals" are simply manifestations of other, more deeply rooted awareness issues.

Are you aware that you can improve? That we can all learn good things from one another? Or do you believe you have already "arrived?"

Awareness and the Retirement Gap

In your *afterwork* years, you no longer operate within the same professional circle of colleagues with whom you once spent the majority of your time. Even the most self-*unaware* person in a business generally had to at least try to be a reasonable person in the office or boardroom, but once you retire, you move outside those etiquette guide rails. You're free to act however you like! You don't need to worry about being fired or causing someone in your company to hold a grudge against you that could negatively affect your future. You can now sound off (in person, on the phone, on social media) as vehemently as you want. In this new season, nobody holds you accountable but yourself—all the more reason to be aware of your behavior and strive to have awareness in each situation.

Another interesting observation is that as we age, we tend to compound in one direction or the other. What that means is that the biases we've built or the rational or irrational mindsets to which we've succumbed are more pronounced when we're older. We all probably know someone who would be considered a wise old sage, who discerns well and has managed losses and wins equally well. Conversely, we all probably know an older person who tends to wreak havoc along the way, saying whatever they want or feel.

> In this new season, nobody holds you accountable but yourself—all the more reason to be aware of your behavior and strive to have awareness in each situation.

As we age, our filters tend to get thinner, and we more quickly manifest who we've allowed ourselves to become. We need to be uber-sensitive to this progression, because a real lack of awareness can bring destruction to many areas of our lives that we might not expect. And the opposite is also true: If we practice awareness well, we can benefit measurably.

The Mental Courtroom

Awareness can be likened to a mental courtroom—except there's a twist. This courtroom isn't orderly; the two sides don't get equal time to argue their cases. Here, the judge allows the plaintiff to make ten statements for every one from the defendant. Yes, it's unfair, but it's the law in this particular state, the "State of Mind."

The plaintiff is Mr. Emotional; the defendant is Ms. Rational. Not only does Mr. Emotional get to talk more, he even gets to raise his voice far above Ms. Rational *and* speak more rapidly without being held in contempt—unless of course you as the judge decide to make that call. That's right, you're the judge. You're the one ruling on every decision in your life.

We should say that no one is exempt from this imbalance. You don't get to change the law of Mr. Emotional having ten-to-one leverage. You merely get to increase your discernment to create the counterbalance.

Let's say someone does something to you that is incredibly irritating. You're ready to bring down the hammer, and you have every right to do so. You wouldn't be incorrect; actually, you would be justified. However, it doesn't mean you should, right?

One of Warren Buffett's many mentors, Tom Murphy (former CEO of Capital Cities/ABC, Inc.), told him early in his career, "Warren, you can always tell someone to go to hell tomorrow." In other words, you don't have to let those words fly today. Buffett said that was "one of the best pieces of advice" he ever received.[60]

We have a simple rule as it relates to email and text messaging. If you find yourself in an elevated moment (and you'll know when you are), go ahead and type that passionate response—but save it; don't send it. Let it marinate for twenty-four hours, then come back and read it again. If you still agree, go ahead and send it.

The funny thing is, the message almost never gets sent. Why? Ms. Rational was allowed to speak. If it's ten-to-one in favor of Mr. Emotional, Ms. Rational needs some time. You eventually discern that even though your points are correct, sending the message won't add any value to your life, so it's time to just let go of the issue and move on. You realize you need to focus on things that will make a good impact in people's lives rather than wallow in life's pettiness. Sending that response could have tied you up for weeks—stewing on it, wondering what the response would be, then responding to the response …

This is only a small example. Often the issues we face that need a heavy dose of awareness are much weightier than a written attack on you. Regardless, the rules of the court are the same. As the judge, you are tasked with creating fair decisions while putting up with an annoying, overheard plaintiff— all day long, all the time. These are the rules under which we have to play the game.

The first major step in being able to play this game well is understanding that the rules are not in your favor. This is called *awareness*, and it's "table stakes" if you are to live a fulfilling and impactful final third of your time here on Earth.

Awareness is when you decide to let the softer rational voice be at least on par with the louder emotional voice.

Just knowing that our rational brain is at a disadvantage is already an advantage. Given a hearing, it can make more sense of many situations. We can even ask ourselves, *Why did I do that? Why did I react that way?* If you know that the voice of discernment (which is something you desperately need) is at a tremendous disadvantage to the voice of ignorance or quick reactions, you're already light-years ahead of everyone else and better equipped to favor your rational side.

Awareness is when you decide to let the softer rational voice be at least on par with the louder emotional voice. Please note, this does not come naturally. Awareness must constantly be chosen; it's generally not something that is learned or obtained. If you learn something, it comes naturally when you attempt it in the future. But awareness will never come naturally.

Keep in mind that this in no way means trying to *limit* your emotions; after all, emotions are fundamental to your existence. It's rather about pausing to understand them and then deciding how to use them, which will create substantial results in your life.

Awareness Promotes Character Growth

So far, we've discussed some methods that will help sharpen your awareness. But let's also explore three character flaws that awareness can help us avoid. In so doing, we'll be less distracted from our purpose.

1. Self-seeking. This takes many forms but is most recognizable within today's social media culture. Reflecting their need to feel valued, people create content designed to bolster their self-image. But this can backfire in the long run. Live instead with the confidence that you are already highly appreciated.

2. Judgment. When we judge others, we are really just projecting who we hope to be on them and holding them to a standard that we wouldn't want ourselves held to. It takes the focus off what we should be working on and displaces it with a false sense of superiority. We're probably better off looking in the mirror first.

3. Excess. Even good things can become bad if there's an overabundance, whether it be food, travel, exercise, relaxation, or work. About four centuries ago, Shakespeare hit on this when he coined the phrase "too much of a good thing."[61]

One deeply ingrained manifestation of excess is mindless spending, which can be outright dangerous for the retiree. Most Americans are accustomed to spending the money they have (and don't have). When it comes to shopping, there's rarely a pause button in our somewhat compulsive retail society. Consumerism comprises two-thirds of the US economy, so we all may be guilty of this one![62]

The issue, however, is not spending or shopping; it's being mindful when you do. Do you really need X, or is it a want? Is the immediate gratification of buying something new worth more to you than the security, flexibility, and impact potential the money would afford you later on? Is the purchase destined to be jammed into a donation bag within a year or two? There's a good chance!

> If you are mindful about purchases, the ones you make will truly be special.

Awareness of spending can be a major hurdle for those leaving careers where the money spigot was always on. Now all of a sudden, their spending comes directly out of a finite trickle of resources. It's an anxious process as they worry about spending but continue their habit of spending unnecessarily.

An increased level of introspection will help you discern what is actually worthwhile and what is frivolous. If you are mindful about purchases, the ones you make will truly be special.

There's no measuring stick without awareness. Good balance is the right solution to any form of excess.

Certainly there are more character traits to avoid than these three; if you can think of a few more that you wish to eliminate, take some time to jot them down. Pull some weeds out of the garden!

Awareness Puts Emotions in Perspective

Seek Help and Wise Counsel

When emotional tendencies (which we all grapple with since they're part of human nature) drive important decisions, the results are often negative. As life marches on and stormy circumstances arise, it can be quite easy to lapse into unawareness, reacting instead of taking a measured approach that leans on getting help and wise counsel along the way.

For example, even at this stage of life, many retirees care for aging parents—uneasy territory where the child slowly becomes the parent and the parent the child. It's not disloyal to tackle this challenge with the help of caregivers when possible. Otherwise you will burn out and make decisions that could cost you more in the long run, including poor health.

Or consider the process of relinquishing your independence by selling your longtime home for the ease and care of living in a retirement community. I (Alex) had a client who, when she was nearly ninety years old, acknowledged she could no longer care for a medically ailing spouse *and* a large home ... she needed help. She shared that she wished to sell her home without a realtor to save fees—despite the fact she was undergoing one of the biggest transitions she had experienced in decades. The process was vexing for her to an extreme degree.

Ironically, she had more money than she could spend in her lifetime. After a frank conversation, she admitted to me that her "Depression-era" mindset could get the best of her sometimes, and she decided to hire a realtor. This professional handled everything, selling her home for a higher price than she expected and, most importantly, reducing her stress and freeing up more time for her to reflect during this emotionally challenging time. In the midst of a life-changing tempest, the last thing you need is the burden of managing complex transactions!

> In the midst of a life-changing tempest, the last thing you need is the burden of managing complex transactions.

Your nest egg is another pertinent example. It's the financial culmination of your blood, sweat, and tears throughout your career. Honestly, how could you not be crazy-emotional and protective of these proceeds you've painstakingly set aside for the future?

Investing and financial planning is a unique, highly complex profession, and the outcomes have long-term, serious ramifications for any household or organization. It's hugely important to get right. But unlike surgery, engineering, law, or rocket science, it's an undertaking that anyone can attempt, and have some luck initially. It's easy to open an investment account, read some articles, and start buying stocks or bonds. It's easy to research social security, estate planning, or retirement accounts and make decisions about what you plan to do.

The problem is that the result can be the same as if you attempted to perform a liver transplant, serve as chief engineer for NASA's Mars missions, or take on the role of lead counsel in a lawsuit. Investing can seem to be easy, until it's not. And when it's not, life trajectories are irreversibly changed.

Awareness of one's own strengths and where one needs guidance isn't as clear with investing and financial planning as it is in other facets of life. But it's just as poignant. If investment management is a true passion and feels purposeful to you, then by all means jump into the deep end. But chances are there are so many other fulfilling activities that you could spend your time doing.

This simple truth about financial awareness is shrouded by so many influences in our society: Classic commercials by large online trading platforms, presenting a super wealthy investor in a beautiful house with a tremendous view, clad in a cozy cashmere sweater and sipping a steaming cup of coffee while clicking a few buttons to achieve trading success. Or the always confounding "financial expert" who wants to sell his or her trading strategy, stock-pick newsletter, or get-rich-quick scheme. The ironic part is if they truly had a treasured strategy or nugget, the last thing they would do is sell it to the world, right?

We are convinced that it's wise to hire a trusted financial professional to help you understand what parts of financial awareness are important and what areas you should avoid. If you don't, you could at best get caught up in something that really doesn't impact the world around you, which is an important source of your fulfillment. At worst, you could make a life-altering mistake.

Balance Fear with Logic

As we've already discussed, we aren't proponents of spending a lot of time in the news. Information disseminated to the public nowadays often seems to have an axe to grind or is motivated by profits. Similar to the tobacco companies' advertisements during the fifties and sixties, much of it is purely fabricated (dangerously so) with an appearance of legitimacy and consensus. It's rare to hear simply the facts. Conclusions and talking points are made for all of us to gobble up and use to frame our life perspectives. It's a depressing state of affairs. The only way to avoid this trap is awareness.

> Information disseminated to the public nowadays often seems to have an axe to grind or is motivated by profits.

But we have a clearer warning: When you feel the walls closing in and the news cycle is especially bad and you know that your investments are down without even looking, it's a good time to stop listening to the talking heads for as long as necessary. It could be three months, six months, or even a year. Turn off the news feed and go outside every day for a walk.

Our minds tend to give in to fear; this is our default bias. The scales are not evenly balanced between fear and logic. They are in fact heavily tipped toward the former. So naturally, when bad things happen, we are tempted to ignore history, which very plainly communicates that yes, bad things will happen, but over time we will recover.

Shelby Davis, who started investing at age thirty-eight with $50,000 and turned it into $900 million by the time of his death, stated, "History provides a crucial insight regarding market crisis: They are inevitable, painful and ultimately surmountable."[63] You also may have heard the coined proverb, "It's not timing the market; it's time in the market."

If we want to worry so much, let's redirect it and worry about how many good things we were able to put in our hearts, minds, and souls this week. What we put in will come out of us, both in words and in actions. If we are careful about what we let in, we'll be less likely to attempt to control the things that are uncontrollable.

Benjamin Graham, the "father of value investing," once said, "The investor's chief problem—and his worst enemy—is likely to be himself. In the end, how your investments behave is much less important than how you behave."[64]

Awareness and Leadership

Earlier we touched on the idea that all of us are leaders, regardless of our role. You don't need to be a CEO to be a leader. If you're a grandparent, you're a leader; if you're post-career, you're still a leader because you have influence over others. The most important quality of a leader is their ability to be self-reflective, or aware—to understand they aren't God's gift to humanity and that they may have some changing to do.

Remember, life isn't about beating anyone; it's simply about a daily pursuit of a better version of you. Show me someone who never changes and has always been stuck in the same old ways, and I'll show you someone who's not only a poor leader but also totally unaware. Awareness serves as our auditor; if we aren't aware, we have no idea where to look to improve.

Key 9: Generosity

If you're no longer working for pay, the idea of generosity can seem odd. Many retirees think, *I've squirreled away this money for the winter—it's all I have. I can't be giving it to something or someone else.*

This reaction is entirely understandable. In a season of life where you still have expenses and a large portion of your livelihood comes from what you've saved, giving some of it away can be scary.

So the point of this chapter is not to make you "philanthropic." That's a term for rich people who donate so they can be recognized. Actually, your generosity isn't needed in order to save the world or even a worthy local organization. It goes deeper than that.

As in so many areas already discussed in this book, we all have a choice to make. We can choose conventional wisdom and use this season of our lives to be "all about us." We can pack away as much as possible and hope it lasts the winter. We can fill our barns to the brim and hope it's enough. In essence, we can rely only on ourselves.

Or we can choose something that's bigger than us. This will entail going up against the worldly force of *fear,* which seems to be the dominant binding agent for those who feel trapped. Giving in to fear is the tendency we need to shatter if we want to have a breakout moment in our lives—where we step beyond our present and into that new future we've longed for but could never grasp. It's the moment when we put a stake in the ground and choose not to be bound by the forces of this world any longer.

Few practices are as effective as generosity when it comes to putting fear in its place. In this chapter we'll talk about being generous in three different ways in your life: (1) giving financially (obviously), (2) sharing your time, and (3) living with a selfless attitude.

Generosity and Your Finances

Money is funny—it makes us act weird. As financial advisors, of course we understand that you need money. Managing money for people is how we make our living, so we're not against it.

But let's talk instead about your *relationship* with your money. If you can manage to view your money as a blessing and a means to facilitate your life's impact, then you're on the right track. However, if you find yourself idolizing your "Benjamins" by checking your investments daily (or perhaps multiple times a day) in order to gauge how you should "feel," you're falling into a common trap.

If the value of your money steers how you feel, it will certainly impact your close relationships. And if it impacts your close relationships, it will steal your joy. And if it steals your joy, then what's the point of having money in the first place? After all, we can't take anything with us when we leave this world, right? Many clients over the years have thanked us for helping them get their mind off their money and onto their future.

By the way, you're not weird for fixating on your money. It's absolutely a natural human behavior. In fact, you're not weird for feeling like you want to even as you're trying not to. Let's face it: None of our lives are as perfect as we may portray. So if you're telling yourself, *I know I shouldn't fixate on my money, but I hear things aren't going well in the stock market, and I really want to check to see how I'm doing today*, be assured that you're normal.

What this book is largely about is understanding that these forces exist and gearing up to combat them so you can stop succumbing to things that add zero value to your life—and lean into the things that will drive true fulfillment.

A Better You

Financial generosity may be the single most powerful catalyst in changing your relationship with the material realm. It is the polar opposite of excessive spending, greed, hoarding, and material attachment. Whatever you give, whether a ten-dollar bill or 30 percent of your assets, it's a resource you are *releasing*. You're intentionally letting go of instant gratification and ownership for the sake of someone else.

The primary force for good in generosity with money is this breaking of control. It's a literal action of trust. It's the antithesis of fear. Generosity is a physical act of giving away the one thing you don't want to give.

> Generosity is a physical act of giving away the one thing you don't want to give.

And what's counterintuitive about financial generosity is that you're the one who actually wins. By giving, you are surrendering the mindset that you have *control* over your money, how it performs, or what it provides. You have moved from control and fear into *trust*.

Many people would say, "I'll give my time, but don't touch my money." And again, we can't blame them for this viewpoint. But financial generosity is still the gateway for releasing the desire to control. As the ancient saying goes, "Where your treasure is, there your heart will be also."[65]

At a recent conference, we heard a psychologist say that after decades of counseling work, he'd learned one truth about each patient's issue: *They were all victims of trying to control things outside their control.* Wow. We both had to plead guilty to doing this. We want to control things just like you do. There is no better way to exit the perceived (but not real) control in your life than to give away some of what is most dear to you.

You may have started this chapter expecting to hear all the ways your money will help others. This is true, of course; you can absolutely make a major impact, which is great news because the world needs more help. However, by being generous, *you* break out of the mold; *you* become more effective; and thus *you* live with increased impact and passion. It's *you* that gets better.

Getting Personal

Much like a physical trainer needs to eat well and practice a healthy lifestyle, we advisors also need to practice what we preach. (It would be odd if you showed up at the gym on January 2 only to realize your trainer was more out of shape than you were!) Following are two ongoing practices that we both implement in our personal lives to stay "in shape" so we can "train" our clients well.

First, we never check our own investments when we want to—only when we need to. For instance, when we need to document our personal annual summaries, perform account maintenance such as a rebalance, or provide financial documentation. Now, of course we know where our money resides, and we'll make a change at any time if necessary. But in general, whenever we have the urge to log in and see what the numbers are, we deny ourselves.

You might say, "I thought I was supposed to check it often. This is what I've always been told." Again, conventional wisdom is often wrong. The more you check it, the more it will own you. We should mention a caveat here: This assumes you are working with a high-quality and trusted advisor. If so, then you're free to abstain from constant checking. You've implemented a good overall strategy, so you can sit back and let it work while you place your focus elsewhere.

What does this frequency of checking your investments have to do with generosity? Glad you asked. The less your investments *own* you, the more generous you can become. It's a self-lifting cycle, not a self-defeating cycle.

> The less your investments *own* you, the more generous you can become.

Second, we give financially on a regular basis. It's the primary metric we both track each year. In our minds this comes first, before any other financial objective, such as savings goals. We're not saying this to get a pat on the back! In fact, in some ways giving can be "selfish," because by being generous, the giver generally receives the lion's share of the benefit. Does that make sense? The giver is the one who gets to escape the prison where money and control confine.

Please understand that you don't need to do exactly what either of us do, or what anyone else does. One physical trainer may have different ideas than the next physical trainer. But the common denominator is that they're both healthy, even if they arrived at that state in a different way. What we're hoping you get from this is that letting go of your control can be achieved primarily through generosity, and the more you let go, the more you'll find yourself pursuing the right things.

Robert Morris is a successful author and Dallas pastor who doesn't hesitate to talk with his large congregation (Gateway Church) about this concept. In his book *Beyond Blessed*, he illustrates how the good life (he calls it "the blessed life") walks on two legs—one is *generosity*; the other is *stewardship*. If you're generous without being a good steward of your resources, you'll hobble all over the place. But if your focus is on stewardship without generosity, you'll be "tight"—a hoarder who never loosens up the purse strings. It's better to walk on both legs.

Robert tells about standing in line at a convenience store while a middle-aged woman in front of him carefully counted out her coins. In a minute he realized she was scraping up every nickel and penny she had to buy $1.32 worth of gas for her car. That was all she could afford.

She wasn't begging anyone for help. She wasn't holding up a cardboard sign. She was truly just trying to get down the road a little farther.

Robert paid for his soda and then followed her out to the pump. "Excuse me, ma'am," he said, pulling out his credit card. "I want to buy the rest of your tank of gas." Her eyes flew open in amazement.

Once the gas was pumped, he pulled a hundred-dollar bill out of his wallet (which he had reserved for just these kinds of moments) and said he wanted to give it her. "But I want to tell you why," he added.

Robert recounted a bit of his own personal story and then concluded, "I'm giving you this money today to remind you that God loves you and has a good plan for your life."

The woman, with tears streaming down her face, hugged him and whispered in his ear, "You'll never know how much I needed to hear this today."[66]

What a terrific illustration of the shape of a healthy, blessed life—managing our resources responsibly so that we have enough to take care of ourselves, plus extra to be generous toward someone in need when the opportunity presents itself.

Playing the Long Game

We look at retirement, or the last third of your life, or whatever you want to call it, as not just the Infinite Game that Simon Sinek describes, but also as a Long Game. When it comes to finances, the Short Game and Long Game have different tenets.

If you've recently experienced a pretty good increase in your account balance, you might be thinking, *I don't know what these two guys are talking about. I'm really enjoying myself, and yet I don't do any of this stuff.* It's a lot easier to play the Short Game and neglect the disciplines (journaling, movement, connection, generosity, etc.) when your net worth is feeling flush and the growth of your investments is beginning to feel status quo. But sooner or later, times of famine will come. The bull market high will wear off, and if you're left with no discipline, you'll find yourself on very thin ice.

> It's not that you can't afford to be generous; it's that you can't afford not to be.

We're not preaching doom here. We believe that over a long period of time, if your financial plan is well designed, you'll be just fine. But having said that, we still need to ask: Will you be prepared for intense seasons of famine if you didn't invest in yourself or practice important disciplines during the feast?

We can respond to that question for you, because we've seen it happen. The answer is no.

So let's change the script and say this: *It's not that you can't afford to be generous; it's that you can't afford not to be.* Here's a very broad generalization: If your financial plan won't succeed with 90 percent of your assets, then it likely wouldn't succeed with 100 percent. Conversely, if your financial plan is going to succeed with 100 percent, then it will likely also succeed with 90 percent. The margin of error isn't that slim.

This observation isn't meant to suggest that there's a set definition of generosity equaling 10 percent; it's simply an illustration. As advisors we build very few plans that are meant to let your final check bounce! It's too hard to thread that needle; we need some room to work. Conversely, we've had more than one client look at a prospective plan and react, "Gee, I don't want to leave all that to my heirs; we should spend more now …" But then even with this knowledge, they think they can't "afford" to give much.

This is evidence that generosity is a state of mind, not an action that's dependent on whether you can "afford" it. If you wait to give until you think you can afford it, you'll never give at all. If your plan is mapped out well, generosity will not torpedo it. Give on.

The truth is that we all can give, whether we have a lot or a little. It's not about the amount given; it's about how loosely you hold what's yours. If you can't bring yourself to be generous, then you're setting yourself up for some serious heartache when times go bad. If you find yourself holding your money tightly, then volatility in retirement will be too much for you to handle.

But trust can do tremendous things for you. By being generous in both good times and bad, you're saying, "It's going to be okay … don't get too excited and don't get too depressed … steady as she goes. I trust the work that's been done … I trust that it's better for me to risk generosity versus clinging to control."

To play the Long Game, we all need our disciplines regardless of how we feel or how our investments are performing at any given moment. We pledge to continue the journey of releasing a little more of our perceived control through generosity.

A Lasting Legacy

We all have a choice in what we do with our financial resources while we are alive. Ask yourself, *What do*

I stand for? and *What do I want the world to look like?* Then seek out and give to organizations or individuals who are pursuing the paths you value. Supporting your own unique vision of a better world, society, or life for someone else can be deeply fulfilling. It's a living legacy that you can start well before you actually pass on a "legacy" in the traditional sense upon your death. While you have breath, you are breathing new life into the world, and you have the privilege of being a witness to that contribution and ultimately its impact.

A living legacy is a remarkable thing. It's the difference between a grandparent saying, "One day I'm going to leave such-and-such amount of money in my trust to each of my grandchildren" versus "I'm going to help pay for the grandkids' schooling now" or "I'm going to do X, Y, or Z for them now and be present in their lives in a specific, ongoing way."

> The time for your effort and generosity is now, not later.

The world doesn't need your generosity at your death; that's the easy way out. If you are worth anything above zero when you die, that wealth will go to someone else. It's inevitable. Waiting for your demise to finally let go of your accumulated wealth is just pure inertia.

The potential for you to make a serious impact starts with cultivating a "today" mentality. Doing so results in the opportunity to see your investment in others come to life. What may have started as a tiny dream or utopian vision can blossom into something momentous—and you can be there to see the bloom! The time for your effort and generosity is now, not later.

The old saying "You can't take it with you" rings true, and chances are that whoever receives your financial wealth once you pass will not share the exact passion, ideals, and world vision that you do. Thus the impact ability of your wealth will be diminished if it's all just bequeathed in the future after you're gone, rather than being put to use now.

Clearly, we aren't against leaving assets and wealth to family heirs or beneficiaries. We help clients every day with their estate-planning decisions, and in fact we enjoy the work. Everybody's wishes are uniquely their own. But the matter of *when* you leave your legacy is worthy of your deep consideration.

Generosity and Your Time

We find it interesting that people treat their money as more valuable than their time, even though we all know intuitively that our time is our most valuable resource. Why is that? Because we can't get more of it. It's limited. You can make more money, but you don't get to make more time.

Having a generous mindset is a posture that comes in multiple forms, much like water is a liquid at room temperature but turns into a solid if frozen and a gas if boiled. Being generous is a mindset that can manifest in different ways. All are equally valuable, but each has a unique contribution to your life. Whereas giving of your finances can free you from being bound to your wealth, serving with your time keeps you closely connected to the world in a humble way.

The two of us have both served at a no-cost grocery store here in Colorado Springs called Crossfire

Ministries. It's funny how before we head down there each time, we feel like we should cancel because we have more immediate things to do. But we've noticed that the longer time passes without our being plugged in, we tend to drift from the benefit of what we experienced the last time we worked there. A little voice inside our heads says, "Oh, you don't need to go do that. You have better things to do. You'll just be wasting your time ..."

We've learned from staying disciplined (meaning we keep serving even when we don't want to) that the voice will ultimately be proven wrong, again and again. So we go. Every time, without fail, we drive out of the parking lot saying, "Wow, we can't believe what others are dealing with." It makes us more thankful for what we have.

> If the benefit of giving money is that you become more trusting, the benefit of serving is humility—one of the greatest single qualities in a human.

If the benefit of giving money is that you become more trusting, the benefit of serving is humility—one of the greatest single qualities in a human. It's really easy to drift away from humility when we run only in the circles we're accustomed to. Sure, it's great that we were able to help a few people at Crossfire who were struggling financially, but to be honest, if we hadn't shown up, the jobs would still have gotten done. So our service wasn't our gift to Crossfire; it was Crossfire's gift to us. We get to spend the next few days with a renewed perspective, and we are able to better serve our families, our clients, and those we rub elbows with daily. We are simply more effective and better leaders because our outlook was readjusted.

It never fails that every time we do this, we are reminded of what's most important. We've never left Crossfire thinking about our investment portfolios or how we were wronged by so-and-so. You won't find us complaining about things we shouldn't (not for a few days at least). It's impossible to see a hungry child with his mom, or load a Thanksgiving box for a family that can't afford it, and keep your focus on yourself.

Dean Merrill, our collaborator on this book, is now in his mid-seventies. He spends every Wednesday morning volunteering at an ESL (English as a Second Language) class for newcomers to America. He's not a professional educator (he's a journalist), but he assists with teaching all kinds of displaced people: young Afghan moms, single guys fleeing the hopelessness of Eritrea, and war refugees from eastern Congo. Together they figure out the quirky language they must master in order to survive in this new country. ("So why does the verb *cook* have a past tense of *cooked*, but the past tense of *go* is not *goed*? Go figure!")

Dean helps set up the room, gets workbooks and pencils from the supply closet, helps students with their worksheets, and leads conversation circles where the students practice explaining how they came to this country, or what "honesty" means to them. For Dean, it's probably the most invigorating three and a half hours of his week.

This is the tremendous gift of serving others, and it's not to be missed in retirement. Otherwise you'll be tempted to stay isolated. Generosity is the best way to get your mind off your problems and focused on being thankful and humble!

Generosity and Selflessness

There's a third, more obscure form of generosity: declining to take what you could have in order that others may benefit. We might refer to this as *selflessness*. This is incredibly hard, especially when we think we deserve a certain reward for putting in the work. But selflessness means choosing to lay down our human desire to receive recognition so that others can be built up.

> The less honor or reward you get for doing something, the more purely generous your actions were.

A lot of times no one will thank you for this form of generosity, which in turn makes it a very generous gift. The less honor or reward you get for doing something, the more purely generous your actions were. You don't have to debate about whether you served just to get a pat on the back or wrote a check only so the organization would honor you. Instead, you can lay your head down at night and feel good about doing something truly selfless.

A great example of this shows up in the ancient story of Nehemiah. He had a cushy job as the cupbearer (butler) for the king of Persia, and he wasn't even Persian. Imagine how hard he must have worked to get promoted to this position, earning the trust of the king of the most powerful empire at the time. But to make a long story short, Nehemiah couldn't forget that his people back home were struggling. So he left what was comfortable and went to lead them … selflessly.

Nehemiah is most famous for rebuilding the broken wall around the city of Jerusalem. But we would argue it was his selfless generosity that should be magnified. See, while the wall was going up under his leadership, he was appointed the provincial governor—an office that came with all kinds of potential perks. I don't think anyone would blame him for choosing to reap a reward for facilitating the rebuilding of the wall; just look at what he gave up. But instead of taking advantage of his new position, Nehemiah used it as an opportunity to model selflessness. He wrote,

> From the time that I was appointed to be their governor in the land of Judah, from the twentieth year to the thirty-second year of Artaxerxes the king, twelve years, **neither I nor my brothers ate the food allowance of the governor.** The former governors who were before me laid heavy burdens on the people and took from them for their daily ration forty shekels of silver. Even their servants lorded it over the people. But I did not do so, because of the fear of God. **I also persevered in the work on this wall, and we acquired no land,** and all my servants were gathered there for the work. Moreover, there were at my table 150 men, Jews and officials, besides those who came to us from the nations that were around us. Now what was prepared at my expense for each day was one ox and six choice sheep and birds, and every ten days all kinds of wine in abundance. **Yet for all this I did not demand the food allowance of the governor,** because the service was **too heavy on this people.** Remember for my good, O my God, all that I have done for this people.[67]

Royalty in that era got a rather significant daily stipend of money and choice food from the people. In an unusual act of leadership, Nehemiah refused, saying the all-inclusive cost of providing this would be too great a burden on the populace. He chose not to take what could have been his so that others could benefit. Now that's the type of leader we want to follow.

We reiterated in the last chapter that everyone is a leader; it's true. But most people who want to be leaders have it backward. Leadership isn't about getting credit or being the "boss"; rather, leadership is stepping out of the way of a reward because you care more about others than yourself. This too is a form of generosity—the generosity of selflessness.

A Final Word about True Generosity

We want to reassure you of this: You don't need a building named after you in order to send ripples across history. Expecting reciprocity means you're still trying to hang on to the power of your donation. It does not equate to fully relinquishing control. Far better to reap the unmatched benefits of openhanded, willing generosity.

Buying a warm coffee for the school crosswalk volunteer on a frigid day can be just as rewarding as writing a huge check to your favorite nonprofit. "The Giving Pledge" is a wonderful initiative—an invitation from Bill Gates, Melinda French Gates, and Warren Buffett asking billionaires to donate the majority of their wealth to charity while they're still alive.[68] But you and I can receive as much personal growth and fulfillment by giving what we can to a church or charity we love. The magic happens not in the magnitude but in the selfless act.

The benefits of generosity aren't measured by the size of your financial gift, or the time spent pouring yourself into others, or the recognition you traded to give someone else a boost in life. Instead, the blessing of generosity is as an emotional feeling that wells up within you when you give freely; it's a sensation of confidence that you are actively engaged in someone or something other than yourself.

> The blessing of generosity is a sensation of confidence that you are actively engaged in someone or something other than yourself.

Key 10: Awe

I (Joel) was aboard a plane on the tarmac at LaGuardia airport in New York, heading home after seeing a client. I've flown a lot ever since I was young, when I was first amazed that these massive metal objects could take me to distant places at thirty thousand feet. I'm still amazed and love seeing the beauty from high above—in this particular instance, the New York City skyline, which never gets old.

But on this day, nearly every person in a window seat seemed to pull out their phone or sudoku puzzle and lower the window shade! Sitting on the aisle, I'm not the type to speak up and ask them to please raise the shade. But I couldn't avoid shaking my head and wondering how our society has lost its sense of wonder.

Too much of the time, we adults have pulled down the window shades of our lives. We're simply not in awe anymore. How much better off we'd be to leave the shade up for just ten minutes, set our phones down, and gaze at the wider, beautiful world. At what point did we stop noticing the mind-blowing features of our planet and let them pass us by without a second thought? When did "important" things in life (our daily routine, our checklist of to-dos) supersede all the awe that's constantly in front of us?

The *afterwork* years are a time when the mindset of "I've seen it all before" can feel like a badge of honor, reflecting one's vast experience. But it's that very mindset that causes someone to become stagnant and inactive. The idea of "that's old news" leads directly to boredom and unfulfillment, because you cease experiencing the new and become rooted in the familiar. You can become jaded against new experience and amazement. Yet the irony is that the true badge of experience is earned when you realize how very little you have *actually* experienced and you strive to encounter more.

> The true badge of experience is earned when you realize how very little you have *actually* experienced and you strive to encounter more.

Humility is a benefit of widening one's perspective beyond "self" and the immediacy of life. When we ponder the beautiful intricacies of the world around us and realize that we're part of a much bigger story, it's hard to see value in mundane pursuits that are hollow and unfulfilling.

A client of ours is a retired physician, now seventy years old, who understandably spent his entire working life indoors—in clinic exam rooms, intensive care units, operating rooms, and hospital corridors. He saw the sun and the trees only when he left work at the end of a long day, or went on vacation.

Since then, he's made up for lost time. If we told you how many of Colorado's fifty-eight "fourteeners" (mountains higher than 14,000 feet) he has climbed, you'd be astonished. If we added how many high-altitude races he has run, you'd be amazed. Why does he do it? Hear his explanation:

> On a superficial level, climbing summits and doing mountain races provides immediate feedback of success. You either stand on the summit or you do not. You either go the distance in a race or you do not.

But there is a deeper, more spiritual reason. I never feel more alive or happier than in the mountains. During a climb, my mind becomes released from the usual worries of life and focuses on the immediate concerns of developing a rhythm of effort that can be sustained for hours; of route finding, snow evaluation, and weather conditions. Winter climbs are significantly more demanding and have commensurate elements of suffering and reward. I need to be able to call on multiple skills during a winter climb, including endurance, rock climbing, and ascending ice with crampons and ice tools.

In *all* seasons, the experience of climbing is one of beauty: the early starts under headlamp before dawn graces the horizon, the warmth of the rising sun, following sinuous ridges to graceful summits, wandering through riots of wildflowers during summer, going up snow couloirs [gorges] in spring, looking out at the empty autumn spaces, and enduring the cold and darkness of winter with the reward of being able to gaze on an endless sea of snow-covered summits. The soul is renewed.[69]

Here is a man who honestly believes the storehouse of awe is not yet even close to being emptied.

An Amazing World

Exploring or living in a beautiful or unique place is undoubtedly awe-inspiring, but the art of finding awe in life can also be as simple as contemplating the vast complexity of the world around us. Roger Penrose, a famous Oxford mathematician and physicist who was a close friend and colleague of the late Stephen Hawking, calculated the probabilities of a universe that would be calm and organized enough to support life. His conclusion? It is a practical impossibility that the universe emerged by coincidence.

It is a practical impossibility that the universe emerged by coincidence.

"This now tells us how precise the Creator's aim must have been: namely to an accuracy of one part in 10 [to the 10^{123} power]. This is an extraordinary figure. One could not possibly even write the number down in full, in the ordinary denary notation" because it results in a "1" followed by more zeros than there are known individual particles in the entire universe![70]

Now take a moment to ponder these additional amazing facts about our universe:

- At the equator, the earth is spinning at 1,037 miles per hour (creating our 24-hour day) while orbiting the sun at 66,627 miles per hour. And our solar system, located in the Orion Arm of the Milky Way, is rotating around the center of the galaxy at approximately 448,000 miles per hour. So as you stand still, just know that you are actually traveling at more than a half-million miles an hour![71]

- The precise tilt of the earth on its axis is what causes the seasons to change as the earth orbits the sun.[72]

- Light from stars takes so long to travel to Earth that when you look at the star-speckled night sky, you're actually peering deep into the past. NASA's Webb Space Telescope views galaxies and stars that are at least a quarter of a billion years old.[73]

On a much smaller scale, think about the billions of particles and cells that make up the intricate systems in our bodies, constantly working in harmony every second as we march through life mostly ignoring it all. Here are some fascinating points to consider:

- If you unraveled all the DNA in your body, it would span 67 billion miles, or 150,000 trips to the moon and back![74]

- If all the blood vessels in the human body were laid end to end, they would span 60,000 miles, circling the earth more than twice.[75]

- Our noses can detect about 1 trillion smells.[76] And if that isn't astounding, a dog's nose has about 50 times the number of receptors! The part of its brain that's dedicated to smell analysis is about 40 times the size of yours, proportionally speaking.[77]

- The human heart beats about 100,000 times a day and about 2.5 billion times in a lifetime, pumping about 1 million barrels of blood—enough to fill three supertankers.[78]

Astounding!

Learning Awe from Children

The realities of the massive and elaborate world we live in are astonishing. On the other end of the spectrum, there is yet another source from which we can learn awe: the humble lives of babies and children.

Every parent remembers how remarkable it was to watch their newborn develop cognitively over the first months, eventually locking their little eyes onto nearby objects, awe plainly visible. They were sensing their surroundings and experiencing emotions for the very first time. No words needed to be spoken to convey how curious and deeply interesting everyday things were to them, like a tree, sunlight, or music.

We can also learn about awe from the concept of childhood and play. Have you ever made a special trip to revisit the home where you grew up? In your mind, it was always an enormous and intriguing place. That gigantic tree in the front yard … the endless miles of green grass with limitless possibilities. But when you returned as an adult holding those nostalgic pictures in your mind, you were surprised by what awaited you.

Recently I (Alex) went back to see my childhood home with its mountainous backyard rising behind. So many vivid memories. However … something had changed. The huge backyard where I spent so much time exploring was now just some scrub oak and rocks on a steep incline. I wasn't thinking about how much fun it would be to take off into the woods again and build a fort or go rock hunting; instead, I noticed how erosion seemed to be eating into the slope, and how some landscaping would improve things.

It certainly didn't seem to be the place of so many epic adventures and excitement and fun I held in my memory and shared in stories with siblings and old childhood friends. In fact, on the surface everything seemed almost laughable in how small and unimpressively normal it all was. Why was my fond memory of the place so different from the reality I was perceiving?

The only part of the equation that had changed was my own mind. It had narrowed to see the world through an adult's banal viewpoint, entirely missing the blissful, playful awe that we all seem to have in abundance before the world teaches us what we *should* be focused on.

Maybe you've witnessed how, when young kids receive a gift, they sometimes unwrap it and choose to play with the box or wrapping instead. Meanwhile, the adults are so intent on having them play with the actual toy that they miss what's going on in the present moment. "Forget the dumb box; look at the toy I just gave you!" they want to say. But the child is caught up in a moment of awe over the box.

You can also probably remember what it was like to head home from a long day at work, feeling mentally spent, hungry, and ready to relax. But if you had children or even pets, when you walked in the door, all of a sudden it was playtime. The interesting thing is that if you allowed yourself to get fully immersed in the fun, you felt rejuvenated afterward. Whether you got down on the floor with your kids, played with their silly toys (so says an adult), sang songs together, or rolled around and wrestled with your dog, it all had the same effect: You were letting your mind unlatch from the never-ending barrage of adult responsibilities. You were de-stressing and getting back to simple basics. You were removing all the "noise" that life constantly threw at you.

Experts agree that even as adults, play is an important element in maintaining our physical and mental well-being.

Experts agree that even as adults, play is an important element in maintaining our physical and mental well-being. Dr. Stuart Brown, a psychiatrist and founder of the National Institute for Play, says that "play is a basic human need as essential to our well-being as sleep, so when we're low on play, our minds and bodies notice."[79] Educator Meredith Sinclair expresses similar sentiments:

> Play is absolutely a mental, physical, and emotional muscle that longs to be used and strengthened.... Not only is it the cornerstone of child development, it also rejuvenates us in so many ways as we age. It's been proven to relieve stress; stimulate the creation of new synapses in our brains.... and increase our overall productivity.... Physical play is incredible and important to keep our bodies (and minds) fit, agile, and healthy as we get older. But if you aren't able to engage in physical play like you once were, all is not lost! The most important thing to aim for isn't a certain KIND of play, but the way that playful experience makes you feel. The kind of beneficial play I'm talking about has no end goals or expectations placed upon it. No trophy you're trying to win or benchmark or striving to meet.[80]

We've talked a lot about being purposeful in your *afterwork* and not just making it all about selfish interests, but deliberately pursuing lighthearted play is still very important. While you'll want to employ the spontaneity that play represents, it's also likely you'll need to be intentional about making time for hobbies, movies and game or bowling nights with family and friends, community events, bike rides, and leisurely walks in the park—as Sinclair puts it, whatever is "for play's sake alone"—"the thing that makes time stand still" and "gets you lost in the process."

Awe on the Run

Clearly it's important to make a place for awe in your *afterwork* life. However, awe is rather illusive; it doesn't occupy a spot on your calendar ("Be filled with awe at 2:00"). It's not quite as precise a habit as movement, or journaling, or showing up for class at your local university. Awe pushes beyond "habit" status and into a state of mind. It's a way of life. It's the window through which you see the world. In fact, awe may be the easiest key of all to use. You just need to remember to take it with you, like your morning coffee when you used to rush out the door to work.

Awe is also a momentum mindset, meaning the more you practice it, the more you want it in your life so it can uplift you. Awe takes your bad day or not-so-ideal situation and puts it into the small perspective where it belongs. Yes, your problems are real, but they are not as big as you think. When you fixate on yourself, you tend to magnify your issues and fears. When you fixate on how small you really are, that you're part of something so big and amazing, you find yourself worrying less. We benefit greatly from the inspiration we take from our awe. There's less stress, less need for control, less "me-itis."

> Awe takes your bad day or not-so-ideal situation and puts it into the small perspective where it belongs.

Even as you enter into your daily routine, driving around running errands or picking up those grandkids, you can shift from a bored mindset to an awe mindset. Notice how the sky may look different ... how the trees come in different varieties or colors ... how the mountains are lit up a different shade of pink ... how the sunset hits the clouds in a new way. Awe can be your antidote to routine.

It's not just about nature. You can gain a sense of awe from a good story, or witnessing your family overcome a difficult challenge, or listening to a friend describe one of their awe moments. If you've been around someone who seems upbeat even when their circumstances aren't what they should be, it's likely they understand awe really well.

This hit me hard when I (Joel) was flying back from my son's soccer tournament in Phoenix. Per usual, a stranger was sitting next to me in the window seat. We didn't do more than exchange pleasantries during the flight. After we landed, I went to grab my bag in search of a piece of gum. I found it, then closed up my bag. As happens to me from time to time, a still, small voice seemed to pipe up, saying in this case, *Offer him a piece of gum.*

I said back to the voice, *But I've already zipped up my bag. Won't it seem a little weird for him to see me unzip it and offer him the gum he just saw me put away?*

The voice clearly said, *I don't care if it's weird—do it.* In my case, I recognized this as God's nudge. I don't profess to hear it all the time, but I know when I do, because often what he asks of me can be a bit uncomfortable.

So I unzipped the bag again, pulled out the gum, and said, "Would you like a piece?"

Guess what he said? "Yes." (Let the conversation begin.)

"So, is Denver home?" I asked.

"No, I'm heading to Kenya today."

"Kenya?"

"Yeah, this is my first time in the United States. I've been here for a week training for my new role."

"Wow, what do you do?"

"I help refugees who are stuck in crisis figure out how to live in the US. My organization has a team that lives here. But I'm over on the Kenyan side, and they want me to understand how it works over here so we can better prepare people before they come."

I have to tell you, in that moment I was in awe. My mind was racing through what this guy deals with in a day—the difference between his reality and mine. As I walked through the airport and drove home, I was unable to shake what a brief exchange had done for my perspective.

I've been practicing awe for a long time. When you do so, it will become more of who you are naturally. You'll notice the flowers and the sunset, but you'll also engage with others' stories and allow them to inspire you. I know this gentleman inspired me.

What if I hadn't listened to that voice and offered him some gum? Who would have been the one to miss out? He acquired only gum—but I gained awe.

Pushing the Pause Button

Like many of the other keys in this book, awe takes ongoing practice. We must intentionally pause our light-speed lives and ponder light-speed itself. Much like the perspective change we experience after attending a funeral or visiting a nursing home, awe can give us a renewed vantage point on our lives, prying open our eyes to truths that lie dormant during the normal ebb and flow of our days.

> We must intentionally pause our light-speed lives and ponder light-speed itself.

Santorini, one of the most popular destinations in Greece, has an interesting cultural affinity for awe. It's a crescent moon–shaped island rising hundreds of feet above the ocean's surface, with whitewashed villages speckling the top edges of jagged cliffs. Looking out on the Aegean Sea from those cliffs, you can see the still-active volcano that devastated the island in the sixteenth century BCE. The whole landscape is surreal.

On the first evening when my wife and I (Alex) were there, we found a quiet cobblestone path with a ledge where we could sit quietly and watch the sunset. As the sky slowly began to erupt in color, we found ourselves surrounded by tourists, restaurant workers, hotel staff, and shopkeepers, who all stopped what they were doing and gravitated toward the cliff's edge to watch the sunset unveil.

We realized (after the second night) that watching the sunset as a community is something the locals value and take seriously. It's a "thing" for them. They actively give it a piece of their lives.

Now, no one would argue that the Santorini sunset should be ignored. But have you ever seen an *uninspiring* or *unimpressive* sunset, no matter the location? Probably not.

The country of Greece is one of the most debt-ridden in the world, with ongoing insolvency issues. Their pension system is terribly underfunded, and they grapple with floods of refugees whenever a new issue breaks out in the Middle East or northern Africa, which is often. So it's not like the residents of Santorini don't have things to worry about. Yet still they pause their lives to soak in the sunset.

If you're still not sure whether awe is a practice worthy of your time, perhaps the following benefits, documented by scientific studies, will convince you once and for all.

Awe …

- Diminishes our inherent self-interest.
- Causes us to become more invested in the greater good and to be more charitable.
- Promotes volunteering.
- Fosters positive emotions such as joy and gratitude, which are linked to greater health and well-being.
- Encourages curiosity and creativity.
- Makes us feel smaller, which helps perspective.

- Improves health, leading to a lower risk of cardiovascular disease, depression, and autoimmune disease.

- Causes time to expand as we savor the present moment and distance ourselves from normal, mundane concerns.

- Sharpens our brains, helping us engage in critical thinking.[81]

You simply need to dial down the volume of your daily life enough to be able to recognize the inspiration that's waiting for you.

It doesn't matter what intrigues you. You simply need to dial down the volume of your daily life enough to be able to recognize the inspiration that's waiting for you. As Gandalf, the wise wizard in J. R. R. Tolkien's *Lord of the Rings* saga, said, "All we have to decide is what to do with the time that is given us."[82] Let a sense of awe start to pervade your consciousness, especially here in the *afterwork* years. You're never too old to reap its benefits.

Part 3

Leaning In and Living Out

Where your treasure is, there your heart will be also.

Matthew 6:21

The Destination We All Share

It was one of the most unique moments we've had in a financial-plan meeting. Jim and Lois were about a year out from retirement and planning to move south of the border. As we do with all our clients, we proceeded to forecast their monetary future.

The program we use has a blue line that denotes the year of retirement, which usually signifies when a person's primary source of income ends and their self-funding years begin. Sure, it's a little scary, but mostly exciting.

Jim fixed his eyes, however, on the second line, which was gray.

"What's that?" he wanted to know.

"That's your death," we responded. "We decided to remove you first in the plan" (as is customary with the men we work with). We thought we would get a quick laugh before moving on, as often happens, but Jim got very quiet. We found out later that our reply had stunned him.

No Time to Lose

When you look at a sheet of paper that lists the dates from your retirement to your death, things get real. Back when you were younger, you could afford to be aimless because you had time on your side. You could say, "I'll figure it out later." But if you enter *afterwork* with that mindset, you can quickly get depressed as time shrinks and your future purpose becomes more elusive.

Yet this stage of life can't be about just "holding on," either, because you have to admit that try as you may, you won't win that battle. Instead, you need to focus on finishing strong with whatever time you have left. Each day must be maximized.

We've also noticed that when people think about their last season of life, they largely discount the last ten years as a lost cause. They imagine they'll be battling health and gravity, confined to their home—or worse yet, a nursing home. But in the interim, they want to push their retirement further out, waiting until age seventy to start social security. They figure it will allow them time to sock away a little more money for what could be twenty to twenty-five years of no earned income. The next ten to fifteen years of that time is their sweet spot, where they believe they'll have good health and capital to make all kinds of good "to-dos" happen.

When you come face-to-face with the reality that your gray line is uncomfortably close to your blue line, it's sobering. It's as if we all know we're going to die one day, but we simply don't believe it. We prefer to live like there's an endless supply of days yet to come. Sure, we've all heard the phrase "Live today like it's your last," but in all honesty, this has no effect on us. We can't afford to actually live like that, right? After all, during our career years, we have too many things we *need* to do that society has convinced us to worry about. So instead, we end up doing all we can to make the next two decades a fairy tale!

Let us restate that there's nothing worse we encounter than a couple thinking that the main point of the next ten to fifteen years is checking off the old bucket list. Not because those items are bad, but because we know that when they're not properly balanced with all the other things we've discussed, that couple will return to our offices in mental anguish that they've wasted a portion of what time they had left.

The bucket list pursuits, in and of themselves, never fill the bucket. This is a desperate place to find yourself—realizing that what you thought you wanted wasn't actually what you wanted.

> Bucket list pursuits, in and of themselves, never fill the bucket.

Changing Our Perspective

Many of us have known someone who has suffered with a terrible health situation or was diagnosed with a terminal illness. The emotional trials of their journey are daunting to us. All of a sudden their mortality quickly comes to the forefront. Every minute they are reminded of the finality of life and molded by a change in perspective as they search for meaning while combating some terrible disease or circumstance.

The light is always more noticeable in the darkness. Their situation begs the questions, *What is truly important to me?* and *What do I feel the need to do before I'm gone?*

Isn't it odd that we can discover immense clarity during such storms? We feel a stronger magnetic pull toward the connections that matter most to us in life. We view each day as being vastly important. Most likely we explore faith more deeply, and our focus becomes pinpointed on what is deeply meaningful.

Now, wouldn't it be wonderful to live this way *without* the specter of sickness or death? How many decades of spectacular living could be had by truly celebrating each moment, not simply following society's grind and getting caught up in the minutiae?

Paul Kalanithi, a Stanford neurosurgeon who was diagnosed with stage 4 terminal lung cancer at age thirty-six, said this:

> In some ways, having a terminal illness makes you no different from anyone else: Everyone dies. You have to find the balance—neither being overwhelmed by impending death nor completely ignoring it....
>
> It is a struggle. The problem is not simply learning to accept death. Because even if you do come to terms with finitude, you still wake up each morning and have a whole day to face. Your life keeps going on, whether you are ready for it to or not.[83]

It's challenging to remove ourselves from the strong currents of our lives to find that balance Dr. Kalanithi spoke about. Most of us are not in an impending death scenario, which is exactly why we completely ignore the brevity of life for now. But indeed, the precious time we do have is finite for each of us. Accepting this truth and acknowledging that the locomotive of our lives is chugging along every second, we have a choice. Do we reshape our approach to daily living through this perspective and live as though time is of the essence? Or do we continue to ignore how quickly our lives pass, until one day we find we've mindlessly wasted our precious time on unimportant pursuits? In that moment of realization, we'll have no recourse to do anything about it!

A New Kind of Bucket List

Rarely is a bucket list loaded with selfless acts of generosity or challenging undertakings that can create lasting fulfillment and personal growth. It's usually filled with special places to visit, relaxing vacations, unique purchases, and epic adventures to be had, with perhaps only a spritz of purpose-driving aspects.

Travel and adventures aren't poor bucket list items in and of themselves, but one should consider why they're there. Most of us have utopian ideas of what we would love to do, but if we stop for a second, write down our list, and ponder each item in depth, we might realize that many are somewhat aimless and empty. At the same time, some might really strike a chord in our heart and soul. So we need to be very intentional about what goes onto our lists, and then take steps to make them reality. If we link our bucket list to the ten Keys, then even our last decade isn't "lost." It's just a different set of circumstances within which to live out our purpose.

> Travel and adventures aren't poor bucket list items in and of themselves, but one should consider why they're there.

One straightforward way to gauge the depth of meaning of items on your list is to ask yourself a simple question: *If I were given only a year to live, which of the items on my list are actually important to me?* Should seeing the Eiffel Tower or golfing at Pebble Beach even be on the same list as taking the grandkids on a special trip, or teaching them how to fish, or joining a nonprofit that works to end modern slavery in Asia? (Some retired clients of ours spend all of their time doing this exact thing.) There are many "wants" in the world, but even more "needs." The needs just aren't as loud and usually don't generate the immediate gratification that a more self-centered bucket list offers. Remember, the world has a way of making the incredibly important seem useless, and the useless seem incredibly important. This is the root premise of the "retirement lie." If we buy this lie, the debt will be too great.

I (Alex) keep a bucket list of sorts for myself, and my wife and I keep one for our family as a whole. We adjust and add items over time as we ponder our lives, who we wish to be, and what our future could hold. It's a very insightful process to sit down with a blank page and write out a bulleted list of the fifty things (or whatever number you land on) you wish to do in your lifetime. It starts out with the low-hanging-fruit desires (hike the Pacific Crest Trail, see the Pyramids), but as you continue to reflect, the philosophical, spiritual, and legacy sides enter the exercise, and your inputs completely change. You may even decide to go back and make changes to the first few you quickly scribbled down as you view them through a more deeply focused lens.

> The world has a way of making the incredibly important seem useless, and the useless seem incredibly important.

Over time, dreams and needs change, so don't feel strange about upending your bucket list as long as you're being true to yourself. We personally have been fortunate to cross a few items off our list already, and we continue to discuss what our true objectives are during our brief time on earth. So much lasting purpose can be found by evaluating your list of lifetime wants and needs, then prioritizing what is most dear to your heart and pursuing it while you can.

We understand that when faced with a short time horizon, the temptation is strong to fill the void through indulgence. But friends, you're not needing to see a certain place before you can be happy. You don't need to be on that beach one last week in order to hit your fill. What you need first is to boldly pursue your purpose and allow these other amazing experiences to be your "garnish" as opposed to your sustenance.

If you try to fill your purpose with awesome experiences, you never will. You'll find yourself thinking, *If I just had that beach home ... or that remote cabin I've wanted. If we had the budget to travel more, then I'd find what I'm longing for.* No, you won't. Not only that, but your retirement budget won't like it either! You can't take a trip that's long enough, you can't relax well enough, you can't ponder on a beach deeply enough. Why? Because you were never made to find fulfillment in the pursuit of self. It's not how you're wired.

The Dash

Imagine this scene: There you stand, facing a stone coming up out of the grass, surrounded by many other stones, with flowers next to each.

Suddenly you realize that what's most fascinating about a tombstone isn't the color, the shape, or the size—it's the dash between the two four-digit numbers. You cannot help but wonder, *Did this person have a marvelous journey? Was it a story for the ages? What actions lay between those dates? If they could come back and speak with us, what would they say?*

"I want to play one more game of pickleball"?

"If only I could travel to one more place"?

"Don't push yourself—you've earned this"?

"As the end nears, do things just for you"?

Hardly. They would be encouraging you with sentiments like this:

You're highly capable, more than you give yourself credit for. You are impactful. You are unique, and the world needs you. So sprint to the finish. Give it all you've got with all you have left in you. Push yourself every day. You don't have to beat anyone; just do *you* to the fullest extent possible. Don't worry about all the stuff you tend to fixate on. Don't let the world tell you what's important; instead, you tell it. Fight for what's good. Reject selfishness, and put others ahead of you.

In essence, they would tell you all the things you need to know in order to flip the script that is easily played out and turn it on its head to produce a life worthy of dreams.

Our absolute favorite thing is to watch a friend or client doing exactly this: living out a beautiful tapestry of balance between *leaning in* and *living out*—a mix of self-disciplines, meeting others' needs, and taking in new and amazing experiences. It may not look exactly like what you dreamed it would, but herein is where the treasure lies.

Cultivated

You may be saying, "Okay, I'm energized to change how I mold my life looking ahead ... but where would I even start?" It's not critical that you implement all the keys immediately to see results in your life. We understand it can seem a bit daunting to get to this point.

A mistake we've noticed over the years as we've attended seminars or leadership training is the desire to change *everything*. It's classic "paralysis by analysis." By wanting to change everything, we change nothing—the task is too involved and too daunting.

It's similar to the feeling you have after listening to a powerful speaker or podcast. You're ready to make changes and tackle the challenges ahead, you sense a new page turning, you feel inspiration welling up within your heart ... until you go back to normal life. Within a day or two, the inspiration has seemingly left the building, and you're back to your status quo.

This happens to all of us. It's human nature to see a new way of thinking or acting, marvel at what it could do in our lives ... and then move on without implementing anything. This

> A downpour of rain doesn't affect a block of granite, but a slow drip over time does.

book is all about rejecting those natural tendencies so we can move toward a fulfilling existence.

There is no one, correct path to take from here except simply to begin. An ancient Chinese proverb states, "A journey of a thousand miles starts from beneath one's feet."[84] All you need to do is progress from where you are now. Take the first step, followed by a second and a third.

A downpour of rain doesn't affect a block of granite, but a slow drip over time does. Water, one of the softest earthly substances, reshapes solid stone gradually through repetitious action. Single droplets impacting an extremely hard, stubborn surface eventually create noticeable change.

We human beings are often like hard stone—set in our ways and skewed against change. It's in our very nature; we are creatures of habit. Any consistent effort we cultivate within ourselves may seem like a meaningless drip in the beginning, but slowly and surely, true change does occur. Eventually we will have been reshaped.

The keys and concepts we've discussed require intentional focus as a starting point. We don't just press a "Go" button to begin disciplines like pursuing purpose in our lives, or enacting true generosity. We need to pause daily and reflect on these ideas to get beneath the surface, down to where true fulfillment is waiting.

If you were to set this book down, cast off your negative traits as much as possible, and use the ten keys more evenly, you'd be taking the most important step in the *afterwork* process. Knowing what the objective is, even if it's not played out perfectly, is far ahead of not knowing who your enemy will be until it's too late. C. S. Lewis said,

> Progress means getting nearer to the place you want to be. And if you have taken a wrong turning, then to go forward does not get you any

nearer. If you are on the wrong road, progress means doing an about-turn and walking back to the right road; and in that case the man who turns back soonest is the most progressive man.[85]

As we have mentioned throughout this text, none of what we discuss is meant to be a box to be checked and moved on from. Each theme is infinite in your life. The goal is to progress toward the light in the distance, to continue to improve and become stronger, better, and more purposeful. There is no end game, no point in time where one masters purpose, or faith, or learning.

> There is no end game, no point in time where one masters purpose, or faith, or learning.

All of these hugely impactful areas are a process in and of themselves. It's a cultivation. A farmer doesn't sow seeds one season and then just sit back for years and reap the rewards. It takes constant effort. Consider the fact that most likely anything meaningful in your life—family, friendships, your connection to the community, even your professional calling in life—they all have a sort of ongoing permanence. They need daily, weekly, or monthly attention. You can't simply achieve them one time and expect the effect to last. You need to cultivate them in and out of season.

The consistency of investing in yourself is what will bring rewards in your life. Keep in mind that constant cultivation can seem challenging at first. It can feel like "work" to remain steadfast in your desire to write journal entries, or be generous, or strengthen connections with people. Just like we discussed in the movement chapter, at first your efforts may seem to drain your energy, but eventually that dynamic changes. You come to realize just how much you need these outlets and undertakings.

Press On!

It's common for people to falsify their retirement as "amazing" when it's far from it. We've seen this firsthand. What motivates them to do that?

Two reasons predominate: First, they are more interested in perception than reality. If others think we have it all figured out, then we convince ourselves that we do. It's a coping mechanism many use to get through this challenging life, but it keeps us feeling okay instead of dealing with the underlying illness.

Second, people are embarrassed about their *afterwork* seemingly lagging in comparison to everyone else's ... so they say theirs is great too. No one wants to be outside the social norm. No one wants to ask, *Hey, what am I doing wrong here? Everyone seems to be enjoying retirement tremendously except me.*

It takes true humility to be honest when it questions the perception others have of you, doesn't it? Pride is so much easier than humility. The best way to avoid risking this conundrum is to make sure your reality and your public profile are equal. If you put the work in on some of these ten keys, your perception will be reality, or at least in much closer proximity.

Whether you're climbing a snow-packed mountain or pushing yourself in some other discipline during these years, it's how you address the challenge that makes all the difference. We know some of the examples we've used along the way seem unattainable to many readers. That's okay; they seem unattainable to us too.

But that doesn't mean they're not useful. These lofty goals call us out of our place and move us more toward who we need to become. Being in awe of what others have been able to accomplish helps us close the gap between where we are and where we can move to. The goals may not pull us all the way there, but even a few feet in the right direction makes a difference. Watching others rise to their individual occasions gives us all a sense of what's possible.

> The secret to activating the ten keys lies in the simple act of not quitting. Press on!

Remember, you don't need to be exactly like anyone. Their goals aren't your goals. Some of us are just trying to get out for a daily walk—forget climbing mountains. But if the knowledge of what others are accomplishing gets you out of the house to go on that walk, then that's the point.

The secret to activating the ten keys lies in the simple act of not quitting. Press on! Yes it's hard, but that's what makes it good, right? How many things in your life are both fulfilling and easy? We all know the answer to that question.

You will absolutely feel like quitting on these disciplines. This is hard work. But of what significance is the reward if the challenge isn't great? The good news is that you absolutely *can* pull these off, and you'll enjoy the journey along the way. It's not like you'll be in a miserable slog here. The more you engage, the more you will appreciate the effort required and the results received. Soon you won't know how you did life any other way.

After leaving the presidency in 1909, Theodore Roosevelt spent a year hunting and adventuring through Africa, then continued his worldwide tour across Europe. He gave speeches along the way in storied places such as Cairo, Berlin, and Oxford. In April 1910 he spoke before a large crowd in Paris, delivering what would become one of his most famous speeches because of this passage:

> It is not the critic who counts; not the man who points out how the strong man stumbles or where the doer of deeds could have done them better. The credit belongs to the man who is actually in the arena, whose face is marred by dust and sweat and blood; who strives valiantly; who errs, who comes short again and again, because there is no effort without error and shortcoming; but who does actually strive to do the deeds; who knows the great enthusiasms, the great devotions; who spends himself in a worthy cause; who at the best knows in the end the triumph of high achievement, and who at the worst, if he fails, at least fails while daring greatly, so that his place shall never be with those cold and timid souls who neither know victory or defeat.[86]

Roosevelt understood the curious idea of perfection: It's in the challenge, not the outcome. Roosevelt's life demonstrated this well: He was the first American to win the Nobel Peace Prize (1906). He facilitated Panama's independence from Colombia so the United States could purchase and construct the Panama Canal expressly for trade and military interests. He also prioritized the conservation of natural resources for the first time, setting aside more land for national parks and preserves than all his predecessors combined, while also creating the US Forest Service and setting aside land for the first national forests.

Roosevelt clearly produced lofty results, but his speech underscores where he saw the value. It wasn't in the accolades and history books; it was in the fight, "the great devotions … in a worthy cause." Do you believe you are in the "arena," or simply watching from the grandstands or the TV?

> Do you believe you are in the "arena," or simply watching from the grandstands or the TV?

You have all the tools at your disposal right now, in this very minute, to rise to the challenge and pursue true fulfillment and a life that is worthy of dreams.

It's your choice: The retirement mirage is there, waving at you in the fog of your future, tempting you to sit in a lounge chair, filling your time with ease and comforts. But the pursuits of purpose, faith, deepening your connections with others, satisfying a hunger for learning, rekindling a sense of awe in life, practicing generosity in its many forms, refocusing your awareness, managing your time as the important commodity that it is, committing to journaling and personal reflection, and maintaining an active lifestyle—all of these in their own unique way will combat the strong societal pressures you face while clearing the path to a fulfilling *afterwork*.

Stones from the mountain roll downhill because gravity takes them where it may. But the mountain itself rises upwards in direct opposition to gravity, pushed by some remarkable force beneath the mountain at its core. The journey ahead for each of us is filled with uncertainty, emotional zeniths and valleys, obstacles, successes, new relationships and experiences. We all are in our own little boats, paddling to stay afloat while being flung around by the sea.

It's not easy or comfortable, but it's real. Treat yourself with gentleness and compassion during this challenging season. If you take the keys we've discussed and integrate them where they will be impactful in your life, there is hope. You'll discover that a dove grasping an olive branch is soaring right above you—and has been with you this entire time.

Notes

INTRODUCTION

1   Dan Buettner, "Emmy-Winning Filmmaker Dan Buettner on Blue Zones,"
    AARP. December 10, 2019. *https://www.aarp.org/entertainment/movies-for*
    -grownups/info-2019/dan-buettner-blue-zones-interview.html.

WHAT NOW?

2   Throughout this book, certain names, places, and other identifiers have
    been changed to respect privacy. However, the essence of each account is
    faithful to what occurred.

3   "American Time Use Survey—2019 Results," *Bureau of Labor Statistics, U.S.*
    Department of Labor. Thursday, June 25, 2020. *https://www.bls.gov*
    /news.release/archives/atus_06252020.pdf.

4   Renee Stepler, "Led by Baby Boomers, Divorce Rates Climb for America's
    50+ Population," *Pew Research Center.* March 9, 2017. *https://www*
    .pewresearch.org/fact-tank/2017/03/09/led-by-baby-boomers-divorce-rates
    -climb-for-americas-50-population/.

5   Jalpa A. Doshi et al. "Depression and Retirement in Late Middle-Aged U.S.
    Workers," *National Library of Medicine, Health Services Research*, 43, no. 2
    (April 2008): 693–713. *https://www.ncbi.nlm.nih.gov/pmc/articles*
    /PMC2442377.

YOU'RE A PERSON, NOT A PORTFOLIO

6   Quote attributed to William A. Ward, "Pennsylvania Avenue Methodist
    Church," *Oklahoma City Star* (May 17, 1963): Page M-110, Post Script,
    column 1.

7   Frank Herbert, *Dune* (New York: Ace Books, 1999), 8.

8   "Guide to Retirement 2022," slide 4, *J. P. Morgan Asset Management.*
    https://am.jpmorgan.com/us/en/asset-management
    /adv/insights/retirement-insights/guide-to-retirement/?gclid
    =Cj0KCQjwpeaYBhDXARIsAEzItbFt1qkRIGZG9H2wkeK6
    _bTC67ZGJB9vrhYcUr5qA0GXpOi9ON5SA9waAsT1EALw
    _wcB&gclsrc=aw.ds.

9   Exodus 16:3.

10 Franklin D. Roosevelt, "Franklin D. Roosevelt's First Inaugural Address,"
    image 1, *National Archives Catalog.* March 4, 1933. *https://catalog.archives*
    .gov/id/197333.

11   Ernest Hemingway, *The Sun Also Rises* (New York: Scribner, 2006), 141.

KEY 1: PURPOSE

12   John McNeece, quoted in Greg Miller, "Creating Cruise Ships with an Eye on Next Generation," *Cruise Industry News Quarterly* 9, no. 37 (Summer 1999): 67.

13   Peter Drucker, as quoted by Bob Buford, *Finishing Well: The Adventure of Life beyond Halftime* (Grand Rapids, MI.: Zondervan, 2011), 280.

14   Adapted and paraphrased from Simon Sinek's presentation at the 2018 Global Leadership Summit.

15   Terry Bromberg, "From Making the Numbers to Teaching the Numbers," *Second Stories: How 10 People Transformed Their Post-Career Lives* (Lansing, MI: Jackson National Life Insurance), 11, *https://www.jackson .com/content/dam/dash/pdf/cmc20462/cmc20462.pdf*. Used with permission.

16   Paula Span, "Many Americans Try Retirement, Then Change Their Minds," *New York Times*. March 30, 2018. *https://www.nytimes.com/2018/03/30 /health/unretirement-work-seniors.html*.

17   Amanda Barnett, "Our Sun," *NASA Science Solar System Exploration*. October 15, 2021. *https://solarsystem.nasa.gov/solar-system/sun/in-depth*.

18   "Your Food Wouldn't Bee Here without Them: What and When Bees Pollinate," *LeaseHoney*. 2022. *https://leasehoney.com/2020/09/01/your-food -wouldnt-bee-here-without-them-what-and-when-bees-pollinate/*.

19   Ed Boling, "2M Beehives Imported to California for Almond Bloom," *The Packer*. February 9, 2022. *https://www.thepacker.com/news/industry/2m -beehives-imported-california-almond-bloom*.

20   Charles Dickens, *Our Mutual Friend* (Hertfordshire, England: Wordsworth Classics, 1997), 540.

21   Rob Cowles and Matt Roberts, *The God of New Beginnings* (Nashville: W Publishing Group, 2018), 15.

22   Paraphrased from Rasmus Ankersen, *The Gold Mine Effect* (London: Icon Books, 2012). Used with permission.

23   Tyler Cowen, "The Five Most Influential Public Intellectuals?" *Marginal Revolution*. January 23, 2018. *https://marginalrevolution.com /marginalrevolution/2018/01/five-influential-public-intellectuals.html*.

24   Jordan B. Peterson, "Narrative, Story, and Writing, Pt. 3," *Dr. Jordan B Peterson Lectures*. March 18, 2022. *https://www.youtube.com /watch?v=ZhEF8RnXKLw*.

KEY 2: CALENDAR

25   R. S. Sneed and S. Cohen, "A Prospective Study of Volunteerism and Hypertension Risk in Older Adults," *Psychology and Aging* 28, no. 2 (2013): 578–86. *https://doi.org/10.1037/a0032718.*

KEY 3: MOVEMENT

26   Elizabeth Anderson and Geetha Shivakumar, "Effects of Exercise and Physical Activity on Anxiety," *National Library of Medicine* 4, no. 27 (April 23, 2013). *https://www.ncbi.nlm.nih.gov/pmc/articles/PMC3632802/.*

27   "Exercising to Relax," *Harvard Health Publishing.* July 7, 2020. *https://health.harvard.edu/staying-healthy/exercising-to-relax.*

28   Phillips Brooks, "Going Up to Jerusalem," *Twenty Sermons* (New York: E. P. Dutton and Company, 1886), 330.

KEY 4: JOURNALING

29   Hal Elrod, *The Miracle Morning* (YoPal Hal, 2016), 84–85. Used by permission.

30   Julia Cameron, "Morning Pages," *The Artist's Way.* April 19, 2017. *https://juliacameronlive.com/2017/04/19/morning-pages-10/.*

31   Rick Warren, "It's Time to Eliminate Negative Self-Talk – Daily Hope with Rick Warren," *LightSource,* May 11, 2017. *https://www.lightsource.com/ministry/daily-hope/devotionals/daily-hope-with-rick-warren/its-time-to-eliminate-negative-self-talk-daily-hope-with-rick-warren-may-11-2017-11773027.html.*

32   Sheryl Sandberg, "Finding Gratitude and Appreciation Is Key to Resilience," *Time.* May 15, 2016. *https://time.com/4336546/sheryl-sandberg-university-of-california-berekley-commencement-speech/.*

33   Sheryl Sandberg, "Sheryl Sandberg Tells UC Berkeley Students What She Learned from Her Husband's Death," *Time.* May 14, 2016. *https://time.com/4336391/sheryl-sandberg-facebook-uc-berkeley-commencement-speech-husband-death.*

34   Paul Petrone, "Why Creativity is the Most Important Skill in the World," *LinkedIn Learning Blog.* December 31, 2018. *https://www.linkedin.com/business/learning/blog/top-skills-and-courses/why-creativity-is-the-most-important-skill-in-the-world.*

35   Used with permission.

KEY 5: FAITH

36   Psalm 103:15–16 NLT.

37   Branka Vuleta, "14 Divorce Statistics You Need to Know in 2022," *Legal Jobs*. January 18, 2022. *https://legaljobs.io/blog/divorce-statistics/*.

38   Elizabeth Gilbert, *Eat, Pray, Love* (New York: Bloomsbury, 2007), 128.

39   Elizabeth Gilbert, "Confessions of a Seduction Addict," *New York Times Magazine*. June 24, 2015. *https://www.nytimes.com/2015/06/28/magazine/confessions-of-a-seduction-addict.html*.

40   Teresa S. Collett, "Being Older Doesn't Make Divorce Any Wiser: Families like Mine Fight to Buck Divorce Trend," *USA Today*. September 6. 2018. *https://www.usatoday.com/story/opinion/voices/2018/09/06/gray-divorce-elderly-couples-marriage-column/1183820002/*. Emphasis added.

41   "Suicide Statistics," *American Foundation for Suicide Prevention*. 2022. *https://afsp.org/suicide-statistics/*.

42   Hebrews 11:1 KJV.

43   Erwin Raphael McManus, *The Last Arrow* (New York: WaterBrook, 2017), 19. Used by permission of WaterBrook Multnomah, an imprint of Random House, a division of Penguin Random House LLC. All rights reserved.

44   McManus, *The Last Arrow*, 19–21.

45   C. S. Lewis, *Mere Christianity* (Harper New York: Collier Books, 1960), 134.

46   Zach Kincaid, "Faith Is a Habit," *The Official Website of C. S. Lewis*. September 18, 2013. *https://www.cslewis.com/faith-is-a-habit/*.

47   Romans 12:9–19, 21 ESV.

KEY 6: CONNECTION

48   Nick Tate, "Loneliness Rivals Obesity, Smoking as Health Risk," *WebMD*. May 4, 2018. *https://www.webmd.com/balance/news/20180504/loneliness-rivals-obesity-smoking-as-health-risk*.

49   Selby Frame, "Julianne Holt-Lunstad Probes Loneliness, Social Connections," *American Psychological Association*. October 18, 2017. *https://www.apa.org/members/content/holt-lunstad-loneliness-social-connections*.

50   Psalm 22:1–2, *The Message* paraphrase.

51   Psalm 23:4, *The Message* paraphrase.

KEY 7: LEARNING

52   Merriam-Webster.com Dictionary, s.v. "surrogate (*n.*)." *https://www*
      .merriam-webster.com/dictionary/surrogate.

53   Roger Abrantes, "Live as If You Were to Die Tomorrow; Learn as If
      You Were to Live Forever," *Ethology Institute.* June 1, 2014. *https://ethology*
      .eu/live-as-if-you-were-to-die-tomorrow-learn-as-if-you-were
      -to-live-forever/#:~:text=Some%20researchers%20attribute%20this%20
      quote,students%20have%20been%20wonderfully%20diligent.

54   Plutarch, *Essays,* trans. Robin Waterfield (New York: Penguin Classics,
      1993), 50.

55   Denise C. Park, et al, "The Impact of Sustained Engagement on Cognitive
      Function in Older Adults: The Synapse Project," *National Library of*
      Medicine. November 8, 2013. *https://www.ncbi.nlm.nih.gov/pmc/articles*
      /PMC4154531/.

56   Alexandre Dumas, *The Count of Monte Cristo,* trans. Robin Buss (New
      York: Penguin Books, 2003), 42.

57   "Graphics for Economic News Releases: Average Hours Per Day Spent
      in Selected Leisure and Sports Activities by Age," *U. S. Bureau of Labor*
      Statistics. 2021. *https://www.bls.gov/charts/american-time-use/activity*
      -leisure.htm.

KEY 8: AWARENESS

58   Jesse Livermore, "Spot the Sucker–It Might Be You," *JesseLivermore.com.*
      2022. *https://jesse-livermore.com/spot-the-sucker-it-might-be-you/.*

59   1 Corinthians 5:6.

60   Gillian Zoe Segal, "Warren Buffett Calls This 'Indispensable' Life Advice:
      'You Can Always Tell Someone to Go to Hell Tomorrow,'" *CNBC.* January 9,
      2020. *https://www.cnbc.com/2020/01/09/billionaire-warren-buffett-shares*
      -indispensable-life-advice-he-learned-more-than-40-years-ago.html.

61   William Shakespeare, *As You Like It* (1623), act 4, scene 1.

62   Abha Bhattarai, "Americans Are Starting to Pull Back on Travel and
      Restaurants," *Washington Post.* June 18, 2022. *https://www.washingtonpost*
      .com/business/2022/06/18/consumer-spending-slowing-economy/.

63   Anupam Nagar, "Shelby Davis' Investment Tips to Achieve Long-Term
      Success," *Economic Times.* August 14, 2021. *https://economictimes*
      .indiatimes.com/markets/stocks/news/shelby-davis-investment-tips-to
      -achieve-long-term-success/articleshow/85324671.cms?from=mdr.

64   Catherine Brock, "How Dollar-Cost Averaging Works in Turbulent Market," *Nasdaq.* July 9, 2020. *https://www.nasdaq.com/articles/how-dollar-cost-averaging-works-in-turbulent-markets-2020-07-09?amp.*

KEY 9: GENEROSITY

65   Matthew 6:21.

66   Robert Morris, *Beyond Blessed* (Nashville: FaithWords, 2019).

67   Nehemiah 5:14–19 ESV; boldface added.

68   *The Giving Pledge,* 2010–2022. *https://givingpledge.org/about.*

KEY 10: AWE

69   Used with permission.

70   Roger Penrose, *The Emperor's New Mind* (New York: Penguin Books, 1991), 344.

71   Doris Elin Urrutia and Elizabeth Howell, "How Fast Is Earth Moving?" *space.com.* January 21, 2022. *https://www.space.com/33527-how-fast-is-earth-moving.html.*

72   Jeremy Deaton, "Summer Is about Here. For That You Can Thank a 4-Billion-Year-Old Rock," *Washington Post.* June 20, 2019. *https://www.washingtonpost.com/weather/2019/06/20/summer-is-about-here-that-you-can-thank-billion-year-old-rock/.*

73   "Frequently Asked Questions Lite," *NASA: James Webb Space Telescope Goddard Space Flight Center. https://webb.nasa.gov/content/about/faqs/faqLite.html#:~:text=How%20far%20back%20will%20Webb,and%20galaxies%20started%20to%20form.*

74   Chelsea Toledo and Kirstie Saltsman, "Genetics by the Numbers," *National Institute of General Medical Sciences.* June 12, 2012. *https://www.nigms.nih.gov/education/Inside-Life-Science/Pages/genetics-by-the-numbers.aspx#:~:text=That's%20how%20many%20feet%20long,round%20trips%20to%20the%20Moon.*

75   DiscoveryHealth.com writers, "Fantastic Facts about the Human Body," *howstuffworks.* February 2021. *https://health.howstuffworks.com/human-body/parts/facts-about-the-human-body.htm.*

76   Sarah C. P. Williams, "Human Nose Can Detect a Trillion Smells," *Science.* March 20, 2014. *https://www.sciencemag.org/news/2014/03/human-nose-can-detect-trillion-smells.*

77   Peter Tyson, "Dog's Dazzling Sense of Smell," *Nova*. October 4, 2012. *https:// www.pbs.org/wgbh/nova/article/dogs-sense-of-smell/*.

78   "Amazing Heart Facts," *Nova*. 1997. *https://www.pbs.org/wgbh/nova/heart /heartfacts.html*.

79   Dr. Stuart Brown, quoted by Jennifer Wallace, "Play Is Important for Adults, Too," *Sunday Morning Herald*. Updated May 25, 2017. *https://www .smh.com.au/lifestyle/health-and-wellness/play-is-important-for-adults-too -20170522-gw9ysw.html*.

80   Meredith Sinclair, interview with David Stewart, "Meredith Sinclair, 52: Let's Play," *Ageist*. June 29, 2022. *https://www.ageist.com /profile/meredith-sinclair-52-lets-play/?utm_source=AGEIST&utm _campaign=b82f2fbfb4-EMAIL_CAMPAIGN_2019_07_19_05_18 _COPY_23&utm_medium=email&utm_term=0_8b785143ba-b82f2fbfb4 -412368229&mc_cid=b82f2fbfb4&mc_eid=963a3811bf*.

81   Christopher Bergland, "The Power of Awe: A Sense of Wonder Promotes Loving-Kindness," *Psychology Today*. May 20, 2015. *https://www .psychologytoday.com/us/blog/the-athletes-way/201505/the-power-awe-sense -wonder-promotes-loving-kindness*.

82   J. R. R. Tolkien, *The Fellowship of the Ring* (London: HarperCollins, 2012), 51.

THE DESTINATION WE ALL SHARE

83   Lia Steakley, "'Stop Skipping Dessert:' A Stanford Neurosurgeon and Cancer Patient Discusses Facing Terminal Illness," *Scope 10k*, published by *Stanford Medicine*. March 11, 2015. *https://scopeblog.stanford .edu/2014/10/20/stop-skipping-dessert-a-stanford-neurosurgeoncancer -patient-discusses-facing-terminal-illness/*.

CULTIVATED

84   Lao Tzu, *Tao Te Ching*, trans. D. C. Lau (Baltimore: Penguin, 1970), 125.

85   C. S. Lewis, *Mere Christianity* (New York: Collier Books, 1960), 36. *Mere Christianity*, by C. S. Lewis, copyright © 1942, 1943, 1944, 1952 CS Lewis Pte Ltd. Used with permission.

86   Theodore Roosevelt, "Address at the Sorbonne in Paris, France: 'Citizenship in a Republic,'" *The American Presidency Project*. Speech made April 23, 1910. *https://www.presidency.ucsb.edu/documents/address-the-sorbonne -paris-france-citizenship-republic*.

Disclosures

This material represents an assessment of the market environment at a specific point in time and is not intended to be a forecast of future events, or a guarantee of future results. This information should not be relied upon by the reader as research or investment advice regarding any funds or stocks in particular, nor should it be construed as a recommendation to purchase or sell a security. Past performance is no guarantee of future results. Investments will fluctuate and when redeemed may be worth more or less than when originally invested. The S&P 500 Index is an unmanaged index of 500 stocks that is generally representative of the performance of larger companies in the US. Please note an investor cannot invest directly in an index.

Interested in using *Afterwork* in your small group?

Access the free Conversation Guide below!